Cat Lovers W⌐⌐⌐ ⌐⌐⌐

"My cat Pickles insisted that I read this. I trust him … sometimes."
—**Nathan the Cat Lady**

"If you have any questions regarding your cat, you should definitely read this book. Your cat will thank you for it!"
—**Gina Gershon**

"I wish I could read this book, but unfortunately, I am allergic to cat books."
—**Kevin Nealon**

"Keeping a cat happy isn't as simple as food, water, and a cat toy. This book is an eye-opener for every conscientious cat person."
—**Brian Cox**

"I love cats because I enjoy my home, and little by little, they become its visible soul."
—**Jean Cocteau**

"What greater gift than the love of a cat?"
—**Charles Dickens**

"The smallest feline is a masterpiece."
—**Leonardo da Vinci**

250 VITAL THINGS YOUR CAT WANTS YOU TO KNOW

Ingrid Newkirk

Book design: Lawrence + Beavan
Chapter start illustrations: Tiani Hernández
Top Tip illustrations: Kim Rountree
Cover photos:
Tabby cat: © iStock.com/nico_blue
Orange tabby cat: © iStock.com/Veronika Ryabova
Black and white cat, brown kitten: © iStock.com/adogslifephoto
Black cat: © iStock.com/hocus-focus

All proceeds from the sale of this book benefit
People for the Ethical Treatment of Animals' (PETA) work
to protect cats and all other animals from abuse.

CONTENTS

FOREWORD
By Kim
Basinger

Ingrid Newkirk is a pioneer in the animal protection world. I have known her for years and consider her not only a great friend to all animals but also a great teacher and partner, as we've worked together on crucial issues that continue to challenge the fight for animal rights today more than ever. At this moment in time, the focus is on our feline friends: cats! And I am delighted to have been asked to write the foreword to her new book, 250 Vital Things Your Cat Wants You to Know. When Ingrid decides to write a book, it will be not just practical but also lots of fun, as she has a wealth of experience and a cool way of presenting new ideas. Light bulbs go on!

I have worked for the protection of wild animals, marine life, farmed animals, and domesticated animals all my life. My mom taught me how to care for and respect all animals, just as I have raised my daughter, Ireland, to do. There were many cats who came through my family when I was young—Bubbles and Black Kitty amongst others—and then in my adult life, Big Boy, Dude, and Pretty Girl. I found Dude in a New York deli by the name of Freedom when he was a kitten. The rats were bigger than him, and he was about to get eaten, so I made the deli owner an offer he couldn't refuse just to get Dude out of there and bring him home. He was the greatest cat who ever lived, but I know everyone thinks that about their cat ☺. Pretty Girl was a feral cat found in a plastic bag in Agoura Hills. The vet called and asked, "She probably won't make it, but would you take her home if she does?" She was a great friend to me but never let me get any work done as she slept right on top of my computer. And SHE was the sweetest cat who ever lived ☺!! Our feline friends come to us in all kinds of ways, but they always make our lives better. Ingrid's book teaches us how we can make their lives better, too.

Along with her playful language and fun pictures that will resonate with any "cat person," it is also delightful the way she gently nudges readers to go beyond the basics. That means to go beyond just throwing some kibble in a bowl and sticking a scratching post in the corner. She encourages us to become real caretakers and friends who are truly worthy of a cat's affection, as cats are very, very special, unique, and magical creatures in so many ways. In other words, when we choose to bring cats into our homes, we have a responsibility to bond with them and to show them that we are worthy of their trust. There are so many fun ways to do this, and this is the guide that will show you how.

All the important cat care topics are covered and much more. If your cat ever goes missing, you will feel very lucky that you bought this book. When you see your cat squinting at you, you will smile knowingly, having learned what that means. And wherever you live, you will most likely make a few modifications for your cat's enjoyment, even after reading just the first chapter.

In no way could you read 250 Vital Things Your Cat Wants You to Know and not be inspired to make some positive changes to deepen the bond, the trust, and the love you have for and with your feline companions. You will help them lead a truly fulfilling life, just the way cats are meant to live.

Oh, yeah, and share it with a friend or two, or—better yet—surprise them with a copy!

ACKNOWLEDGMENTS

A cat book wouldn't be possible without cats, so the first big thank-you goes to all the cats who have brought me joy and taught me important things about themselves, including Oreo, who was rescued by PETA after a teenager posted a video of himself repeatedly boxing the cat in the head, causing him to lose part of an ear.

I am also thankful to Patti Breitman, not only for her professionalism but also for her kindness; to Janet Mills, who understands and helps cats and other animals; and to Debbie Goodman for her support of our work.

Thanks, too, to present and past PETA staff members, including Karen Porreca, Gray Caskey, Marcy Dalton, Alisa Mullins, Karen Johnson, Alison Green, Carla and Karin Bennett, Danielle Moore, Lisa Lange, Mindy Gregg, Bobbi Hoffman, Robyn Wesley, Emily Rapp, Chrissy Matthies, and everyone who shared their cat experiences with me, including my parents, Hilly and Anthony of Lawrence and Beavan, and Maria Peterson (who created the most cat-respectful private home I have ever visited).

And thanks to everyone on PETA's clinics and on our emergency response, Community Animal Project, and cruelty investigations teams who have pulled cats out of trees and sewers, provided emergency care, sterilized thousands of cats from low-income homes, helped shut down laboratory experiments on cats, and worked with law enforcement to have cat abusers arrested and convicted.

Thank you, too, to all the PETA staff and volunteers who've acted as servants to the cats in our guest rooms for a night or two and to the "BP oil spill cats" who fled Louisiana to call our Norfolk, Virginia, headquarters their permanent home.

Finally, thanks to the companies and individuals responsible for all the goodies, from wisdom to toys, that help us make sure that cats are healthy, happy, safe, and loved.

WHAT WILL THIS BOOK DO FOR YOU AND YOUR CAT?

This book, 250 *Vital Things Your Cat Wants You to Know*, has two simple but important goals: to make your cat happier and, as a result, to make you happier, too.

Over the years, I have shared ordinary, extraordinary, happy, and heartbreaking experiences with cats. The pointers I've picked up should be as useful to you as they have been to me—from tiny tips, such as which scratching posts are most likely to save the sofa from being shredded, to big ones, such as how to find a beloved cat who has suddenly vanished.

This book was written with the cat's perspective in mind. Cats, like us, want to be comfortable, loved, stimulated, and fulfilled. They dislike being uncomfortable, lonely, bored, and frustrated.

"Anthropomorphism" is an old-fashioned word. Most people are too embarrassed to bandy it about these days, although in the past, everyone from hog butchers to people who practiced pigeon bowling (yes, it's just what it sounds like!), drowned kittens in a sack, or knocked giraffes unconscious to measure the thickness of their ears used "the A word." They were all a little too anxious to convince people that cats and other animals do not experience "human" feelings like pain—a recognition that might just have stayed the hand that carried Kitty to the well or, for that matter, liverwurst to the lips.

Today, most people have watched enough *National Geographic* specials to remember what we learned in Biology 101—that we are all members of the animal kingdom. It is one great orchestra of life, and joy, fear, love, and amusement are not the exclusive territory of Homo sapiens.

Some of my favorite life lessons came from a cat named Moomin. When I first took her in, she was a tiny, frail Siamese kitten with a respiratory virus that left her with a wheeze you could hear a mile away. There were other cats on the premises, but she was instantly drawn to the only other Siamese. Jarvis was handsome but reserved— to the point of snobbishness.

I doubt Moomin realized that she, too, was Siamese. No doubt she was drawn to Jarvis because he looked just like Mom and Dad. This lonely little kitten pursued him relentlessly. But every time she pulled her tiny wheezing body up to his, he swatted her across the face, spat, and headed for higher ground. Yet no matter how often he moved, no sooner had he settled down again than along came Moomin, squashing herself right up against him, certain that, at any moment, Jarvis would recognize her as "family."

After about a week, Jarvis gave up. He began to let Moomin sit beside him while still ignoring her. After a few weeks, I caught him grooming her. From then on, they did everything together: ate, slept, and once, in a fabulous feat of coordination, simultaneously threw up on my shoe.

After Jarvis died 14 years later, Moomin spent weeks roaming the house at night, crying for her lost love. Their relationship taught me something quite obvious: Togetherness is a wonderful treasure—for cats as much as for humans.

Togetherness does not mean ownership. "Own" is a word that doesn't work when it comes to cats, and not only because they are such independent beings. "Own" is a word that describes something like one's relationship to a pair of sneakers, but the idea of animals as possessions makes anyone who truly respects animals flinch.

Sure, this book is mainly about how to create unbridled happiness in your cat, but I'll have missed my mark if it does not also make you think about your relationship with all animals. This book will make the case that we should treat every last one of them not as things but as individuals with an inherent right to be respected, even when they noisily bring up a hairball during a dinner party.

You will find the tips on these pages both practical and enriching, no matter what. If you have a cat or are contemplating sharing your life with one, this book is for you. If you know someone else with a cat or who is contemplating sharing their life with one, this book is for them. Please pass it on—or better yet, buy another one just for them.

ANYONE CAN BE
A TERRIFIC CAT
GUARDIAN

Lots of people already do a good job in that role but want to know more. Others care *about* cats but may not have a clue how to care for them. Even in the homes of diehard cat lovers, I've met cats who were literally screaming for the right kind of attention and cats who had thrown in the towel and become as withdrawn as caterpillar grubs— *and their people somehow didn't notice there was a problem.*

Some of us, like me, do occasionally wonder if cats are a superior species. I mean, look at them. They are far more reliable, better behaved, more attentive, and much cleaner than most human beings. I'm sure the condition of my house sometimes scandalizes my cat— especially when I'm working on a complex project and the whole place starts looking like a garage sale in progress.

Look at your cat. As if expecting visitors, your cat is always up in the morning, appearing well rested, washed, and groomed. At mealtimes, you never have to shout, "For the umpteenth time, will you come and eat?" Cats are fastidious about their litter boxes, they try to keep their claws filed down, and they rarely snore.

Miraculously, despite this evidence of their superiority and our numerous shortcomings, cats seem to find us endearing or, at least, amusing servants. They are rarely critical, and if we're very good (or really pathetic), they may deign to snuggle up to us, a sensation as delightful to a "cat person" as a dip in a pool on a hot summer day.

There are ways to shamelessly capitalize on this feline bonhomie and the fact that a cat, being of a polite and grateful nature, will give credit where credit is due. This means that when you apply the advice herein, your cat will not only love you despite your inadequacies but also admire (yes, admire!) or even worship you.

Perhaps there is no greater proof of how "human" other animals are than the realization that they can even lie! Cats do it, of course, but consider the true story of one young American Sign Language–taught chimpanzee who accidentally broke a toy. Not realizing he was being observed through one-way glass, he decided to cover up his role in the mishap. When his teacher entered the room to ask, "Did you break the toy?" the guilty baby shook his head vigorously, pointed to another chimpanzee baby, and signed, "No. *He* did!" I'm sure you've noticed how cats, who adore knocking things off other things, often stare at you, eyes wide with innocence, if you happen to hear the crash and come running.

Come to think of it, it's a wonder cats will have anything to do with us at all, considering the impositions we have placed upon them throughout history. Remember, we have thrown cats aboard ships to act as unpaid rat catchers on perilous ocean voyages and buried them alive in tombs as favored possessions. Perhaps our ancestors were too busy trying to invent central heating and stud poker to treat cats with the respect they deserved, but that's no excuse for burning them at the stake (as was done during the Salem witch trials!), tying their tails together to make them fight (a beloved 18th century sport to which people brought their knitting), or, as was done in Europe, celebrating St. John's Day by sewing cats into sacks or putting them in wicker baskets.

Our behavior today isn't that hot, either. In hundreds of laboratories, cats are still treated like disposable test tubes with tails, and there are millions of abandoned strays scrounging through trashcans looking for sustenance and often finding only the cold and moldy leftovers of someone's dinner.

Caring about cats as you do makes you a very special person, perhaps far more special than you realize. Your cat is very lucky to have you. In fact, I wish all cats were so lucky. Not everyone has your level of commitment.

Visit your local animal shelter and you will find it bursting at the seams with cast-off cats. Wonderful, well-behaved, attractive cats are sitting there waiting for you. Those cats didn't wake up one day and decide to play Russian roulette with their lives. They woke up one day to find their family had decided to give them the old heave-ho. Humans can be incredibly cavalier about their obligations. When cats get old, sick, or inconvenient, some people dispose of them, only to replace them with shiny, new cats—as if these dear souls were of no more importance than used lightbulbs.

Well, whatever your outlook, if you follow the suggestions on these pages, you should be tickled with the results. Adoring eyes will follow you wherever you go. And the purring may get so loud you will have to buy earplugs. You will feel like a movie star.

What greater reward could anyone who loves cats hope for?

1
HOME
SWEET
HOME

Or is it? Could it be that your cat is living one of her nine lives in a human-oriented dwelling place and, worse, living at ground level? Let me elaborate: Before cats belonged to human beings, they belonged to themselves. They answered to no one unless they felt like it. In fact, before 18-wheelers and human beings got into the act, cats had no natural enemies to speak of except parasites, and even then, they knew which plants to chew on to fight off illness and even managed to pass on their folk remedies to their youngsters.

Yes, cats used to be self-sufficient in those halcyon days before we, if I may borrow Joni Mitchell's lyrics, paved their paradise and put up a parking lot. Cats also got along perfectly well, thank you very much, without can openers and litter boxes. Sure, they probably wouldn't have said no to a catnip toy, but their lives were full without such artificial stimulants.

They were whole, dignified, free-roaming, independent souls. They carved out their own (often vast) patches of turf, defended them with their own teeth and claws, enjoyed a social life with friends and family, had the opportunity to flirt and to select and reject suitors, raised their kittens, provided balanced meals for their families without benefit of advice from nutrition experts, and still had time to play "pounce." We humans were about as necessary to their existence as a bowling ball.

Now look at modern Kitty's confines. Your cat is probably stuck inside a wood and cement box with compartments, otherwise known as your home.

Before you protest, "But I live there, too," chances are that you leave your house or apartment a lot. Sometimes you are in and out the door so fast that your cat's image of you amounts to a big blur. Sometimes you are out and about so much that your cat can't remember what you look like.

Out there in the real world, you see things your cat would give an eyetooth to see. You interact with others of your own kind, even if that only means swearing at the driver in front of you who brakes for falling leaves. Your brain and body are actively engaged, perhaps greeting neighbors, waving to a fellow jogger on a trail, or even making change.

Meanwhile, your cat is back home, staring at the wall. At least, your cat *should* be indoors when you're not conducting supervised leisure or exercise time, because today's outside world is a dangerous place for a cat. Don't imagine it is not. It is full of traffic and strangers with candy in their pockets who want to take your cat for a little ride (see chapter 10). This means your cat is virtually a shut-in! Your home is his entire world.

Take a look around Cat World. Unless you live somewhere like Hearst Castle, there's probably not much to it from a cat's perspective. This calls for action! You have to fool Kittums into thinking you and she live in the most interesting place on Earth. You have to enrich her otherwise drab little life.

2
CREATING
A ROOM
WITH A VIEW

First and foremost, whether you have spacious gardens or a squinty little view of a junkyard outside your window, cats must have comfy places to sit and look out. To the dedicated bird-watcher, nothing makes the time pass quicker and the whiskers twitch faster than the object of her natural, abiding interest and careful study.

While outwardly cats may appear aloof, just below the surface they are like that nosey neighbor in *Bewitched*. Provided with a view, your cat not only will have something to distract her from resenting your absence but also may actually figure out exactly who that handsome man is who visits the house up the street.

Ordinary windowsills are usually too small to accommodate even svelte feline bottoms. A cat likes to survey her domain while stretching or lounging and does not like to be seen wobbling about while moving from one strategic lookout point to another. As they age, cats tend to model themselves after Renoir's women or Chubby Checker. Skinny windowsills just won't do.

HOME IMPROVEMENTS

The Best Fix

Bob Walker, a San Diego architect, showed the way by incorporating a 110-foot (not a misprint) carpeted, elevated catwalk into his house. If you didn't look up, Bob's house could seem normal, but if you did, wow! The catwalk wound its way through several rooms at cat-perfect, near-ceiling height. It incorporated resting boxes, curving staircases to run up and down, peekaboo cutouts into cupboards and adjoining rooms, and more. The cats watched everything from up there, including the Walkers, their dog, and TV. Yes, cat fur floats down, so the vacuum didn't have to be taken up.

Walker's cat-friendly house, which took him and his wife, Frances Mooney, 10 years to perfect, was quite fancy. The house was later sold and all that wonderful catwalkery was dismantled, but you can still see it here: PETA.org/Cathouse. The less artistic or ambitious among us can certainly make more modest constructions that will please felines to no end. Don't miss the catios, cat enclosures, and even ladders in the Handy Resources section at the back of this book.

Lesser Measures

Get out your band saw or call a carpenter and replace that tightrope job with a windowsill at least a foot wide. Cover this renovation with 2-inch-thick foam rubber, then add soft but thick cushioning (nail it down so it doesn't move around or fall off), a thick piece of padded (of course) carpeting, or if you subscribe to *Architectural Digest* or *Better Homes and Gardens*, material that matches or complements your curtains.

If your cat is already a bit of a blimp, you may need to install a ramp up to the ledge or platform. Otherwise, strategically placed furniture can do the trick.

The Easiest Solution

Drag a bureau, a bookcase, or another solid bit of furniture over to the window and firmly attach to it a padded seat (e.g., a cushion or covered foam) to create hours of viewing pleasure.

Cat Tree

Buy a cat tree like the large catnip variety from FELIX (541-668-

0696) or PETA.org/Felixtree. A tree is particularly satisfying because, of course, before cats were deprived of their real, natural lives, they lived and lazed about in trees, and to this day, they carry a tree-lounging gene. Make sure your faux tree is positioned close enough to a window and in such a way as to allow Kitty a dignified posture and a good view without causing her any eye or neck strain.

For Extra Credit
- The more scenic viewing spots, the better. Windows are "cat TV," and if there's nothing playing on one channel, it's nice to have another to switch to.
- Place a bird feeder near the window in winter and spring. (Birds should not be fed year-round—it foils their ability to forage.)
- Try to catch the sun by providing at least one east- or west-facing "cat-bird seat." Cats long to sunbathe all year long!
- Oh, and if Tiddles is occupying a dining room chair at dinner time or your favorite lounger during prime time, you wouldn't be so mean as to move him, would you? I thought not. Thank you.

Turn a Set of Ikea Bookshelves Into a Catio

Cats long not only to look outdoors but also to go outdoors, and that can be too dangerous, as I point out in chapter 14, but there are ways to make the outdoors accessible while keeping your cat safe. Here's how: PETA.org/Catio.

LITTER BOX ALERT

As you would wish to find it—that's how a cat's litter box should always be left. Of all the indignities cats suffer at our hands, having us in charge of their litter box arrangements is one of the worst. Cats' noses are sensitive, and their urine can be pungent. They do not wish to soil their dainty feet in it. So never fail to remove solid waste at least twice a day, and always remove it immediately if you notice the cat has just been in the box. A truly happy cat never has to wrinkle his nose—the litter pan is completely dumped out *no less frequently than once a week*, swilled with vinegar, washed with soap, and then thoroughly rinsed and dried. Sometimes a little baking soda is placed under the litter. In multicat households, there is at least one pan per cat plus one. Oh, how sweet life can be!

To be absolutely sure that your cats' litter is free of chemical

TOP **TIP**

Never use a pine-based cleaner. It can be toxic to cats. And although "clumping" litters are convenient, you should know that some experts think clumping *clay* litter may do to Kitty's innards what it does to household plumbing, that is, block it up. Writer Marina McInnis relates how three kittens deteriorated from a "robust, healthy group" to "thin, dehydrated little skeletons" with claylike bowel movements that had the consistency of the clumping litter they were using. The stools even had gray and blue flecks in them, just as the litter itself did, and smelled of clay. She says that only emergency medical care—a holistic treatment that included slippery elm bark and lots of broth—saved them.

deodorizers and other stuff, you can use alfalfa-, coconut-, or corncob-based litters or natural clay types, some of which use chlorophyll. At PETA, we love our corn cob–based litter, which is easy to clean. There you have it.

Some Etsy shops sell nice cabinets that provide the following advantages: They help keep dogs from foraging in the box, can reduce litter tracking, and are attractive, so they can be kept in convenient locations rather than being relegated to bathrooms (which are closed while people bathe, etc.), basements, and the like. Obviously, handy people could also make their own.

SERIOUS HOME HAZARDS

A home should also be a haven, not a place where a cat needs a hardhat and steel-toed boots. Check your place for these hazards, rather than discovering them too late:

- *Electrical cords.* Unplug anything heavy that could topple over and injure a playful cat or kitten who decides to play with the cord.
- *Recliner chairs and fold-a-beds.* Cats like dark places and beds and find them perfect for hiding out or pondering their navels. Cats who are caught in the mechanism when the chair or bed is opened or closed can be seriously injured or killed.
- *The dryer.* Always, always, always check inside the dryer before turning it on (see chapter 15).
- *Cords.* Cats love to play with curtain and blind cords, but they can easily get all wrapped up in them and strangle. Coil the cords up to the top of the window and pin them there with a clothespin.
- *Bags with handles.* Cats can become stuck in the handles and panic. If this happens when you are not home, the cat may be injured or killed. Keep such bags out of reach of cats, or cut handles off.
- *Stovetops.* Gas or electrical stoves can present problems. Use burner covers. Most cats stay away from anything they realize is hot, but you may wish to train them away from the stove by

gently spraying them with a tiny bit of water if they try to jump up.

• *Conventional antifreeze.* It contains ethylene glycol, which is poisonous. Just a teaspoon can kill a cat. Antifreeze should never be left lying around, but for extra safety, buy Sierra, which is less toxic and made with animals in mind. It's available at PETA.org/Sierra, or you can call 1-800-323-5440.

3
HOW TO EXCITE KITTY'S MIND

Cats are thoughtful, clever, and innovative. Without stimulation, they can become ill-tempered, bored, and resentful. They need things to play with, to figure out, and to think about, or they will go quietly nuts, just as you would.

It doesn't take an animal rights activist to notice that big cats stuck in cages at the zoo or in those appalling traveling shows that sometimes visit shopping malls are neurotic. Many suffer from what behaviorists call "zoochosis," which means animal neurosis. Animals in danger of losing their marbles develop back and forth, 'round and 'round movements, such as pacing and circling, and use them in the same way people chant mantras: The repetition creates a rhythm and a pattern that can help the brain escape powerful stress and endless frustration.

Cats need, desire, and appreciate satisfying challenges, particularly during kittenhood and adolescence (but not only then). After a day of stimulation and challenge, they can collapse in a contented heap beside you when you get home from a hard day at work.

TOP **TIP**

While Kitty can play with some toys alone, both species will miss out on maximum fun if you don't use those that demand your personal involvement.

A toy chest is not only somewhere to stow Kitty's stuff but also eventually a treasure trove of old favorites to reminisce over as Kitty gets all gray around the whiskers.

SIMPLE AND CHEAP THINGS YOU CAN DO

If you lived in a dirt patch without a dime, you could scrounge up things your cat would value more than all the fancy stuff you might buy. Discarded feathers and leaves, a handful of grass (beware of pesticides), dried flowers, and empty boxes or twigs would keep your cat occupied, as well as keeping you in stitches. Here are some simple and cost-free but adored amusements.

- Teach your cat to imitate a golden retriever: Scrunch up bits of tinfoil and roll them into balls, then toss and flick them around. Cats can be pretty adept at pouncing on, retrieving, and eventually amusing themselves for hours with these shiny silver toys. Bobbi Hoffman, a teacher, tosses paper balls down the stairs, and her cat, Kiwi, bounds down and proudly brings them back to be put in play again, just as a dog would return a thrown stick. Other people use pinecones or nut shells. The PETA office cats enjoy retrieving little dime-store plastic lizards (which, believe it or not, they must recognize as lizards, often chewing off their tails and dragging them around in their mouths, looking mighty proud).
- Cats have been known to inhale unusual substances that make them start doing the cat equivalent of giggling uncontrollably. Jack, one of the PETA office cats, adores shoes. Should someone slip theirs off under a desk, he can be found upside down with his head stuck inside it and a really silly grin on his face. Richard Vialls of Lancashire, England, meanwhile, is trying to determine what is in the ink of the New Scientist magazine. His cat slobbers all over his copies of it and then nuzzles into "the revolting mess," clearly getting high.

A sure bet, however, is catnip. You can buy starter catnip and grow it in the garden, a window box, or indoors under greenhouse lights. (Keep the seed packet handy for when your local police officer drops by—the leaves look a lot like marijuana, and that's not legal in all states yet.) Then stuff whole or ground-up leaves into a square of cotton material, perhaps cut from an old T-shirt. Or when you've given up searching for its mate, shove some catnip into the toe section of a sock, add some cotton wool or any sort of safe stuffing, and then tie this newly made ball off by knotting the top of the sock. A piece of string tied to it will allow you to drag the old sock enticingly about the floor, or it's just as wonderful given to your cat as is.

Most cats will roll on their backs, purr, and gaze dreamily into space with one of these mildly stimulating sachets between their paws. Wouldn't you *love* to know what they are thinking at such times?

A Super Catnip Crazy Pants Cat Tunnel is available at Walmart, and you can get a catnip scratching post on Amazon.

Bored with catnip? The people at The Cat House (8 Castle Pl., Cochrane, AB, T4C 1G4, Canada, 403-228-2287) suggest trying honeysuckle. Cats agree, behaving ludicrously in its presence—drooling over it, rolling on it, smiling like dolphins at it, just as they would with the "C weed." They sell a variety of honeysuckle products.

- Create a "bag of tricks" by placing an empty paper grocery bag (handles cut off, if there were any) on the floor. When Kitty enters the bag, which is inevitable, sneak up and move your fingers lightly along the side. Using several bags will provide rapid-fire hiding places during finger attacks. If you are otherwise engaged, your ever-imaginative cat will still find the bag amusing sans fingers. And a tiny peephole cut in it will be put to use, too. (Empty cardboard boxes are also appreciated.)
- Recycle the pull tab from juice containers—into a cat toy. Don't ask me why, but most cats will play with these little doodads until they keel over from exhaustion.

- In the evenings, try dousing the lights and running the beam from a pencil flashlight or a very low-wattage laser pointer over the carpet (not near the cat's face) and up the wall. As with all games, do let the cat win sometimes.
- Here's one of the few ethical uses of a fishing pole (although a long stick works just as well): "Cast" a piece of string out toward your cat, having secured a bit of fluff, a plastic worm, or another squiggly bit to the end, and reel or pull it back in—for hours.
- Finally, walking on the beach or in the park? Don't forget to pick up feathers, seaweed, a crab carapace, and other interesting but harmless discards that your cat will find smelly and fascinating to play with. (I dry seaweed first and then tie it to a doorknob or to a string and drag or dangle it about.) A few feathers tied together make for a super game of "pounce on the prey." One of the office cats cherishes an enormous box of feathers in which she rolls, purring, every day.

OFF THE SHELF

Now, here are a few toys I'd recommend dipping into the, er, *kitty* for—and you can find them all online.

The Cat Dancer

Amazingly simple yet absolutely tantalizing, the Cat Dancer is a twizzly bit of fluff on the end of a flexible wire that you twirl around and is available on catdancer.com. Some people cheat and tie it to a doorknob, which can work well, but cats far prefer having you attached to one end of it.

The Incredible Cat Tunnel

The PETA office cats go rabid for cat tunnels, which they use as an instant amusement park the moment we throw one onto a floor. Most of them weigh nothing and collapse to less than nothing, so you can toss them in a drawer—but they unfold into a flexible net hiding-and-peeking-out-from place that can be curved around corners or laid out straight. A huge variety is available on the internet.

The Cat Track

This is a fabulous, fascinating, and thoroughly annoying Ping-Pong ball in a plastic container.

Cosmic Catnip Scratching Post

Whoever marketed this is a genius and a rich one, I'd guess: It is basically a brick of corrugated cardboard with a bit of catnip rubbed on it. However, as soon as claws meet paper, even the most sedate cats seem to "dig."

Cat TV

These videos of flitting fish, birds singing their hearts out, and all manner of interesting animals putting on *The Gong Show* for cats meet mixed reactions from feline audiences. Some cats can't get enough and almost meld themselves to the screen, fascinated; others yawn and nod off the way people do when faced with the umpteenth rerun of *Gilligan's Island*. Our cats like the one called "Video Catnip."

The Really Silly Ball

I call it that, and of all the ball toys, the one our cats like most is Bojafa's smart cat ball from Amazon. It comes with an interactive LED light that makes a cat do a double take. There are endless games, toys, and distractions available on the internet, of course, and the more you look at them, the more you can determine that, if you have the time, you can devise many of them at home with a little DIY innovation.

4
AVOIDING PERIODONTAL DISEASE

According to a veterinarian affiliated with Southern California Veterinary Dental Specialties, "By 2 years of age … 70% of cats have some form of periodontal disease." How has this happened?

Traditionally, kitties have kept their mouths fresh and teeth clean by chewing fresh, raw grasses and gnawing on the bones of rodents who couldn't sprint well. Today, it's mostly mushy food (even dry kibble turns to mush in the mouth), so teeth are vulnerable to decay and gums to infection. (The first sign is bad breath, but periodontal disease can lead to serious systemic infections.) The modern cat's teeth (30 per cat) sometimes shred! It's not a pretty sight, and it's painful for puss, to boot.

I once knew a parrot who had been kept in a cage in a dental hygienist's office. This poor bird had endured a miserable life, not only deprived of other birds to preen and talk to but also forced to endure a steady diet of piped-in show tunes! For four years, she watched, all day, every day, as a person in a white smock plopped people into a chair and cleaned their teeth. When she was finally liberated from her life as a living ornament, this smart bird couldn't wait to try her "hand" at dentistry. When the aviary door was open, she would fly over to the nearest human being, hop onto their shoulders, and pry open their mouths, all the better to insert her beak into those hard-to-reach nooks and crannies! As disconcerting as this could be for unsuspecting visitors, they had to admit she did a fine job!

The parrot doesn't make house calls, so here are three easy things you can do:

1 If your cat is still a kitten, start his tooth-care regimen in the privacy and comfort of your own home. Gently rub your finger along Kitty's gums and teeth. Use a little garlicky water if you like (crush a clove of garlic into ¼ cup lukewarm water). Do this as often as it is tolerated, once per day or week.

As the little nipper grows, you may wish to pick up a bumpy, plastic finger guard from your veterinarian or sneakily substitute an extra-soft toothbrush while practicing your very best cooing bedside manner. The important thing is to stimulate the gums and rub away the grime and slime. You can use toothpaste but not much—you won't want to leave any residue in Kitty's mouth. Some people believe plantain leaves make a good cat mouthwash. Here's the rinse recipe: Steep a tablespoonful of leaves in ½ cup boiling hot water for 5 minutes. Strain, cool down, and use as a mouthwash. Use twice a day for 10 to 14 days.

Alternatively, use the herb in the morning and apply vitamin E (fresh out of the capsule) to the gums with your fingers at night. (This treatment is very soothing.)

Many cats are finicky about most types of toothpaste and

TOP **TIP**

If you notice that your cat's gums are bleeding or if your cat starts to chew slowly or eat out of only one side of his mouth, something is undoubtedly amiss and your prompt attention is required.

absolutely *loathe* mint flavoring. In fact, some cats will bite their human companion's lips if they smell the stuff. There are exceptions, of course. Loretta Hirsh, former president of the Washington Humane Society, had a ginger-and-white "baker's cat" named Jasper who *adored* mint and liked his chin rubbed. No fool, Jasper found how to enjoy both pleasures simultaneously by standing on the bathroom sink and rubbing his chin over the toothbrushes in the wall holder. (The Hirshes reported that Jasper also loved to roll olives along the floor using his chin!)

2 Have your cat's teeth examined by a veterinarian at least once a year or immediately if you detect difficulty eating or see the cat pawing at her mouth. Should your cat have to undergo *any* procedure for which anesthesia is required, seize the opportunity to have his teeth professionally cleaned!

3 A Petrodex Dental Kit for Cats is readily available online.

5
KEEPING CLAWS NEAT AND TRIM

Cat scratch fever doesn't have to mean a choice between shredded couches or "off with their claws!" Cats *have to* scratch. We may not know all the reasons, but among them are the needs to mark territory, condition their nails, play, and exercise. Even proper stretching requires scratching. So while it's important not to prevent cats from scratching, you can control the where (if not the why).

Declawing is like taking a hatchet to a hangnail. It is illegal in England, not because the land of my birth is a nation of eccentrics but because the operation is decidedly cruel. In fact, the British Veterinary Association calls declawing "an unnecessary mutilation." In North America, all bona fide animal protection organizations frown on the procedure and a growing number of veterinarians refuse to declaw.

Contrary to most people's idea, the surgery involves severing not just nails but whole phalanges (up to the first joint), including bone, ligaments, and tendons! Possible complications of this surgery include pain, damage to the radial nerve, hemorrhage, bone chips that prevent healing, and recurrent infections.

According to veterinarian Dr. Nedim Buyukmihci, "Declawing is unacceptable because the suffering and disfigurement it causes is not offset by any benefits to the cat. Correcting deficiencies in the cat's environment is the appropriate course of action."

Dr. Nicholas H. Dodman of Tuft's University School of Veterinary

Medicine reported, "I find the declawing of cats abhorrent and inhumane." Dr. Louis J. Camuti, a practicing vet for more than 40 years, puts it this way: "I wouldn't declaw a cat if you paid me $1,000 a nail!" 'Nuf said!

One Cat Fancy magazine reader wrote, "Can you please tell me why my five-year-old Persian no longer runs and plays since being declawed? It's been eight weeks since surgery. Before being declawed she was full of life; she played ball and ran and jumped with me every day. Now all she does is sleep and eat. It's very sad to see a cat who was once so full of life now so lifeless. Do you have any idea why she is like this now?"

How I wish the writer could turn back the clock. What she is seeing is that the scars from declawing are not only physical but also psychological, because "doing their nails" is as normal to cats as stretching. If their natural instinct to manicure is thwarted, they can go a bit cuckoo.

Some cats get so shell-shocked by declawing that their personalities change and they simply refuse to use the litter box again, proving that there's more than one way to ruin furniture coverings! One theory is that when they use the box after surgery, their feet are so tender that they associate their new pain with the box permanently. Another is that because they can no longer mark with their claws, they mark with

TOP **TIP**

You may need to assist young, naïve, or habituated cats by calmly and gently disentangling their claws when they start scratching on something precious, carrying them to the scratching post, and helping them get started by making scratching gestures on the post with their paws. If you react to a mistake with harsh words, screams, or threatening body movements, this can backfire, hopelessly souring Kitty on other suggestions you might make.

urine instead. Whatever a declawed cat is thinking, the results can be unpleasant. Other declawed kitties become so traumatized by this ugly, painful, and unethical surgery that they end up spending their maladjusted lives perched on top of doors or refrigerators, out of reach of real and imaginary predators against whom they no longer have any adequate defense. They lose their grip on reality, seeming unable to concentrate on much beyond the loss of their nether bits, their vulnerability, and their feelings of betrayal.

Chris Lewis of Rockville, Maryland, almost lost his declawed cat, Pharaoh, when the cat lost his footing while walking along a balcony rail and fell several stories to the pavement below. It is true that an innovative veterinarian once outfitted an injured police dog with a stunning new set of glass teeth, but sadly, no cat who has lost her mittens has had a replacement lot sewn on. Chris now keeps the balcony door firmly locked.

Yes, declawing involves removal of parts of cats' toes. This is a problem because cats actually walk *on their toes* rather than on the balls of their feet as humans do. If you watch a declawed cat, you will see that some of them move like slightly inebriated drivers trying desperately to walk that chalk line for the nice trooper who has pulled them over for "weaving." That is because they have a hard time balancing properly on their stumps. Gone forever is that wonderful, assured, "catwalk" gait the supermodels mimic at the haute couture shows in Paris.

It may be easy to see the difference in how a declawed kitty moves, but what we *can't* see is worse: The nails can actually grow back *inside* the cat's paw, causing pain but remaining invisible to the eye. Declawed cats need regular X-rays to monitor this potential problem. Whether or not the nails grow back, declawed cats can suffer chronic back and joint pain as shoulder, leg, and back muscles weaken. No wonder cats suffering in this way may bite when scratched or stroked too hard.

Is there a solution? But of course!

Unless she spends most days playing in the road on the hard pavement (which one sincerely hopes is not the case), Kitty's claws will have sharp hooks on them. To prevent furniture damage, that hook simply needs to be carefully snipped off or blunted.

You can get Kitty to do the job herself, or you can lend a hand.

Simple and Free

- Get thee to the nearest patch of woods, the beach, or a gardening store; linger a while and enjoy yourself, then bring home a nice stump. Naturally, foragers can't be choosers, but if you can get your mitts on a chunk of tree that's about 18 inches in diameter and 3 to 4 feet tall, Kitty will be able to stretch her claws up on it nicely and then sit atop it afterward.

  If the world's perfect stump is not in evidence, settle for anything: Any stump is better than no stump at all. To get the resident bugs out of it, leave it outside, exposed to the sun and off the ground. After about a week, bump it around a little bit outside to dislodge persistent insect squatters and drag it indoors, preferably placing it on an easy-to-vacuum surface or some newspaper.

  Your mini-tree is now ready for Kitty to dull her nails and pull off old growth ("sharpen" is a misnomer), exactly as nature intended.

- In the same way sharks can detect a drop of blood in a mile of ocean, cats' sensitive noses can pick up even very faint odors. So, smear a drop of cologne or flea dip on any material Kitty is fond of tearing up and she will probably veer away from it like a jet fighter at an air show.

• You can also deter cats by temporarily covering off-limits furniture with something slippery, such as contact paper. If it's left on for a while, cats will move on to something else (hopefully, something you don't mind being scratched) and forget that that was their favorite spot. It's a good idea to put a scratching post near where they normally scratch (at least for a while if it is an inconvenient location) and, like the soldiers at Dunsinane sneaking up on Macbeth, keep moving it gradually to a more convenient spot.

A note to parents of infants and young children: Don't worry needlessly that your cat will seriously scratch a child. Cats are generally careful around children—recognizing them as vulnerable, part of the family, and potentially naive—and sheath their claws even during play. All should be well unless you put the cat in a position in which she must fight for her life against an unsupervised and unruly child strong enough to try to squash the breath out of her torso or disjoint her tail. Mothers can worry about all sorts of things, but freak accidents aside, cat scratches aren't usually among them. Please be sure to talk to your children about treating cats with care and respect, of course.

Simple and Cheap

Many cats love shredding paper (and playing in shredded paper), but if you prefer not to have your home covered with shredded paper, try these solutions:

• Rustle up a serviceable cat scratching post by covering

> ## TOP **TIP**
> You can also spark your cat's interest in a scratching post by sprinkling it with catnip, hanging toys from it, and playing with her on and around it. Keep her interested by sprinkling new catnip on it weekly. (Try having Saturday "catnip parties"! Fun for everyone!)

a wooden or plastic box with carpet remnants and anchoring it by putting sand, a cement block, or bricks inside at the base. Or buy or make some scratching posts (three is not a crowd). There are also scratching boxes made of cardboard or sisal. They lie flat on the floor and are cheap enough to scatter about. One favorite is the Cosmic Catnip Post, which is available at PETA.org/CosmicCatnip. Don't forget to leave a post or scratching box near your kitty's favorite nighttime sleeping place. Cats love to do a yoga stretch and then scratch their nails when they wake up.

In the Johnson household, Jasmine and Ariel have persuaded their people to staple carpet samples (about 2 feet by 3 feet) onto the wall near door jambs starting at about 6 inches off the floor. This allows a good stretch and scratch while allowing them to keep an eye on two rooms at once.

Vertical posts should be sturdy and tall enough for a cat to stretch out fully (a wobbly post can frighten a cat away). It can also be covered with sisal or a rough-textured carpet turned inside out. Cardboard posts need to be changed when worn out or your cat will lose interest.

TOP **TIP**

Unless major surgery is required, never leave Kitty overnight at the vet's office, no matter how nice everyone is. Your cat depends on you to err on the side of guarding her against nasty goings-on. Every humane officer has horror stories about "what went on in the back" of even respectable-seeming clinics, e.g., crates were stacked to the ceiling during a holiday rush, animals were forgotten after surgery, a fire broke out. Bring Tiddles home.

• Invest in a decent pair of cat nail clippers (available from your veterinarian and from pet supply catalogs and stores). Make sure they are kept sharp.

Cats' claws must be *carefully* trimmed. Press the paw between your fingers and thumb to unsheathe the claws. Trim just enough to blunt them (about ⅛ inch from the tip) but not enough to cut the quick, which, if you are lucky, can sometimes be seen outlined within the nail, ending between the tip and the bend. Only do Kitty's front paws. Hind paws pose no threat, except during cat ninja kicking contests, and will help Kitty climb trees to safety if she accidentally slips out the door. Weekly trims are recommended. Have your veterinarian give you a "how to" demonstration the first time if you feel a bit shaky.

Here are the three steps to follow:
1. Press to extend the nail fully.
2. Calculate where to cut to avoid the quick.
3. Trim firmly and decisively. (He who dithers about makes trimming more traumatic, plus nails may snap unless the cut is strong and firm.) Try hard not to traumatize your cat.

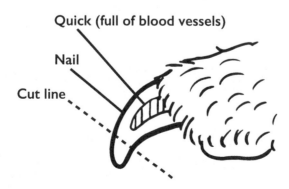

Quick (full of blood vessels)

Nail

Cut line

Easy

Take your cat to the veterinarian for regular claw trims.

Even in the best of veterinary hospitals, the scents and noises as well as the understandable fear of the unknown make even sophisticated, worldly-wise cats worried and scared. It is worth messing up your own life a bit to stay at your cat's side during the procedure, thus minimizing the trauma of an attack by strangers wielding metal objects. Then, whisk Kitty straight home, apologize profusely, and lay on a really nice treat or six. All may be forgiven. *May.*

Some nice scratching post suppliers are here: Felix Katnip Tree Company (PETA.org/FelixBeam) and Cosmic Catnip Scratching Post from Cosmic Pet Products (PETA.org/CosmicCatnip).

Soft Paws are nail caps for cats, soft pieces of vinyl that keep cats' nails blunt and harmless four to five times longer than routine nail trimming. The durable caps are held in place by an adhesive and are available in sizes to fit kittens and adult cats. The nail caps usually last four to six weeks, depending on the rate of nail growth and the activity level of your cat. They are easy to apply and safe for your cat. They can be ordered at PETA.org/Softpaws.

6
OUT WITH THE WORMS AND FLEAS

Emergencies, like finding that your cat has cleverly managed to wedge her bottom into a firewall, are not the only health and well-being concerns that demand our prompt attention. Case in point: the matter of internal and external parasites. These little devils do not visit cats in the benign way pilot fish perch on sharks' heads or little birds enter hippopotamuses' mouths to pick their teeth clean. Symbiosis is not up their alley. Theirs is a one-way street. Worms and fleas simply besiege cats and make their lives miserable. Luckily, dealing with them will not break the piggybank, and they are no big deal to tackle—but tackle them we must.

MORE THAN A PAIN IN THE NECK

To look at it one way, the universe is a complex system of interdependency in which one organism clings to its fragile existence through its interaction with another organism. To look at it in a slightly different way, some people spend their lives mooching off others. To a parasite (no slight intended), a cat represents a cozy, warm place to live and a 24/7 open buffet. External parasites, such as fleas, invite their friends, such as tapeworms, to move into the part of the house they're not using, i.e., your cat's intestines. In fact, they actually pack for them: Flea larvae eat tapeworm eggs and Kitty sometimes inadvertently ingests fleas when she cleans her coat, so the eggs get a safe ride through the digestive tract protected by the flea's body and end up in the intestines, where they hatch and turn into adult worms.

If enough parasites call Kitty "home," they can cause severe problems, such as anemia, especially in tiny kittens and elderly cats (look for white or pale gums)—but even a small squatter's camp means blood and food are being taken away from your cat, and such conditions as dry skin, stomach pain, and irritation from flea bites are offered in their place. As soon as you see even one flea or one tapeworm segment, serve an eviction notice.

RID ME OF WORMS, PLEASE

If you live in the South, the best advice when it comes to tropical storms or external parasites is to up and move. However, internal parasites flunked geography, so you can't escape them even if you hightail it to the snowy peaks of Colorado. In fact, giardia, a protozoan parasite, thrives in some of the prettiest rivers there.

Luckily, you can usually deal with most internal parasites all in one go, whether they are hookworms, roundworms, or tapeworms. Then there is the aforementioned bug giardia, which can be detected using a special test. Coccidia, another protozoan, is often hard to detect at all.

Cats can pick up parasites from a mud puddle, the soil, another cat, or infected meat or greens. Hookworm larvae are particularly insidious. They can simply burrow quietly through normal skin when you are not looking. These are all good reasons to keep Kitty indoors.

Many worms are invisible to the naked eye, and others are so small that even people under 40 who have never experienced the humiliation of squinting at a canned goods label can't see them without a magnifying glass. Others, like tapeworms, are impressively long but are tucked away where you can't find them, although tiny segments of their bodies break off and may be seen wiggling momentarily in your cat's stool or dried into a tiny white flake, stuck on her rump, pretending to be a grain of rice. Roundworms, which are common in kittens and often give a bloated beach ball look to a small cat's stomach, are visible if passed in feces. They resemble strands of Silly String.

Outside the body, all worms and worm segments die quickly, but worm eggs are resilient and can lie in wait in the grass and soil for a long, long time, until that special moment when the possibility of reinfestation becomes a reality for them.

If you see any of the symptoms of parasitism, such as diarrhea, blood or mucus in the stool, bloating, a stomach sensitive to the touch, pale gums, a dry hair coat, or malnutrition, you'll no doubt act immediately. But just to be sure, no matter how shiny-coated and energetic your cat may be, take a sample of his stool to your veterinarian. The sample should be recent, say from within 12 hours, unless you have refrigerated it.

The vet will examine the sample under a microscope and let you know what desperate little life-forms have taken up residence inside your cat. It is always possible that you'll be told your cat is worm-free when, in fact, he isn't. That means adult worms weren't in the mood to make eggs the day you collected the sample. Since seeing evidence of tapeworms is a hit-and-miss proposition, your vet will gladly accept your suggestion that you want to worm your cat anyway.

Perhaps most important, mark your calendar in big letters and do not miss the re-worming date. The first worming kills the mommy and daddy worms, but larvae must be killed after they have hatched and before they are ready to bear their own young. That makes the second worming crucial.

SHUTTING DOWN THE FLEA CIRCUS

Summer, especially in Southern states, can be very depressing for non-fleas. Like college students on break, flea conventions flock to enjoy the warm weather and have no compunction about partying it up year-round, making your cat scratch so much he looks as if he has Saint Vitus' dance.

Controlling fleas requires a multipronged approach.

Anticipating your less-than-welcoming response to their presence, fleas will have taken precautions to secure their territory, cleverly invading not only your cat but also your carpet and gaps or cracks in the floorboard or tile where they can lay the eggs needed to produce future flea armies. All their hiding places must be treated at the same time, when you de-flea your cat.

Attack the infestation in four areas: your home (now their home, too), your lawn, all bedding, and your cat.

Your Home

Spring cleaning may have been invented to thwart fleas. Vacuum the rugs, and clean cracks in tiles, floorboards, and any crevices daily during spring and summer months. Once you start looking for flea hideouts in your home, you will probably find so many gaps in the construction that you will no longer be amazed at your winter heating bills. Do not let the filled vacuum bag sit around, even for a moment. Quickly take it and its cargo of fleas and flea eggs outside and put it in the trash, otherwise fleas will walk back out the way they went in and their eggs will hatch in the nice warm bag.

To kill larvae, go room by room sprinkling borax, diatomaceous earth (from any garden or pool store, but be sure it doesn't contain chemical additives), or ordinary table salt on the carpet; let it sit overnight; and then vacuum it up the next morning.

You can use a good flea shampoo in a mop bucket or commercial rug cleaner to kill whatever bits and pieces of animal life are left behind after you vacuum. Rinse thoroughly afterward, because these products are strong and strong-smelling. They can be unpleasant, even toxic, to a cat or kitten.

Tuck cedar blocks and/or herbal sachets between the cushions of upholstered furniture.

If you choose to "bomb" your house with a commercial preparation, read the warning later in this chapter about poisoning—and for added safety, please be sure to keep your cat(s) away for twice the amount of time listed on the label and to meticulously clean/rinse away any chemical residue.

Federal authorities decide what goes on these labels and are too often beholden to the industries they are supposed to regulate, and they are not known for their accuracy in counseling citizenry on the use of hazardous substances. Think how cheaply you can buy a home in Love Canal; remember their assurances that Agent Orange–like insecticides could be sprayed from aircraft or sprinkled on breakfast cereal; and remember how they laughed off concerns about exposure to DDT and joyously lined children's school ceilings with asbestos.

The Outdoor Breeding Ground

If your cat goes out onto your lawn, you might use an organic flea control product there, too. Some contain nematodes (microorganisms that eat flea larvae) and can be sprayed or sprinkled on grass and soil. These are safe for animals, including birds, humans, and "friendly" garden dwellers such as earthworms and ladybugs. They can be found in pet stores and in the lawn and garden sections of hardware stores and supermarkets. Read labels carefully.

The Bedding

Put all the cat's bedding (which includes window seat covers and your own blankets) into the washer and wash it on the *hottest* water setting with a flea shampoo *that advertises that it kills the eggs*. If in doubt, wash everything twice. If fleas reappear, launder bedding once a week.

The Cat

And now for the centerpiece of all this activity—the cat.

You can go the natural route, which is less toxic and usually far safer for your cat (although even these applications have been known to cause nasty reactions), or you can take your chances and the cat's and bring in the heavy toxic artillery to "nuke" the fleas.

Whichever way you go, try not to leave your cat at the vet for a flea dip or bath. Do it yourself, with help from a cat-conscious assistant if you can get one. That way, you will not have to worry that your cat has suffered a reaction that has gone unnoticed or has been left too long in a cage dryer by a busy attendant. Buying the dip or shampoo yourself means you can read the label carefully (please do) and choose the product you think is best. By the way, never bathe your cat if you don't *have* to, but if you *must* (for example, if he gets covered in soot after an ambitious run up the chimney or a sudden bang causes him to jump into a bowl of barbecue sauce), always use a nonslip rubber mat in the sink or tub. Being set upon with water is one indignity; not being able to keep your footing is another. Take a hint from Heloise, who advised that, in the absence of a rubber mat, you can place a small window screen on a couple of towels at the bottom of the tub, allowing your cat to hang on while being bathed. Also, run the water before introducing cat to tub. Unless your cat is an Asiatic fishing cat, which is just what it sounds like, chances are he is scared to death of that gushing noise.

Danielle Moore once lived with a cat named Bean who would sit on the kitchen counter while she washed the dishes. Bean would

TOP **TIP**

If flea bites and scratching at them have your cat's skin raw and inflamed, Avon's Skin So Soft could help. Mix 1.5 ounces of Skin So Soft into a gallon of water and use it as a shampoo. It has soothing properties that cat people swear by. Aloe vera can also be used to calm down hot, itchy skin and is harmless if licked off. And an added benefit is that it repels fleas!

reach over and place her paw in the stream coming from the faucet. Sometimes she would climb right into the sink and allow a slow flow of water to fall over her head! She was fascinated with water and would perch on the edge of the tub while Danielle bathed. (Not that Bean jumps into the tub—she doesn't.)

Bean was found under the hood of a truck. Before driving home one evening, the driver had thought she heard a cat meowing. She searched all around but Bean didn't call out again, so she figured the cat had run off. She drove nearly 30 miles, on the expressway and on city streets, before arriving at her suburban home. Later that night, her son walked by the truck and heard the cat. Opening the hood, he found Bean perched precariously near the motor. When he lifted her out, she was trembling, but she immediately began to purr in his arms.

The next day she went to live with Danielle, still covered with grit and grime. That's when Danielle learned to bathe a cat the easy way, using a towel swaddling. Here it is:

Gently wrap the cat in a towel, in the manner that one might swaddle a newborn baby, with the feet secured and the head uncovered. A very good idea is to sew two towels together with one side left open to form a bag. Cats usually don't mind being swaddled as long as it is done gently. Don't wrap too tightly, just enough so that the cat can't flail about and slide in the wet basin. (There are also mesh bags that you can use to slip your cat into to allow you to control him during the bath. The bags can also be used to help restrain a cat for medication or manicuring and are available on Amazon, made by YLONG.)

The temperature should be pleasantly warm, not hot, so that the placement into the water is almost imperceptible to the cat. Put just a few inches of water in the basin. Fill a couple of large pitchers with warm water for rinsing. Cats never like being sprayed, so don't even think about trying to turn on the faucet to rinse them off. This should all be done as quietly as possible.

With the cat's head uncovered, place him in the sink. Allow him to "get his feet wet," and speak to him in a soft and reassuring voice. With your hand or a sponge, get the towel surrounding the cat wet. Don't splash. Work a gentle baby shampoo through the fabric. Don't get the cat's head wet. You can use a sponge or washcloth on his head later. Don't work up the sort of lather you might when washing yourself. You don't want to take too long rinsing. The towel can be used to massage the lather all over the cat.

To rinse, pour the pitchers of warm water ever so slowly over and under the towel. As more of the lather is rinsed away, gradually push the towel down and away from the cat. When he's all rinsed, gather him up right away in a fluffy towel and pat him dry. He'll want to get away from you to groom himself, so make sure he has a warm place to sit and dry off.

A Toxic Shocker

The active ingredient in most commercial flea products is a pesticide called imidacloprid. Every summer, poison control centers receive thousands of calls reporting flea pesticide poisonings of cats and dogs.

When you read most pesticide labels, you will find warnings not to get it on your skin, to wash your hands after applying it, and to keep it away from children. But the label goes on to give directions that usually include rubbing the substance into the animal's coat—as if his skin would not absorb chemical poisons, too!

At PETA, we obtained a video of a tiny calico kitten in a laboratory cage, crying and experiencing body-racking convulsions in a flea shampoo test for a well-known manufacturer. Believe it or not, just because the kitten suffered doesn't mean the company decided not to market the product! As with many industries, the litmus test of whether or not to sell something is sometimes whether or not the company can outsell the amount of money it has to pay out in damages when consumers bring lawsuits!

One example of a potentially toxic product that was tested on animals yet appeared on store shelves is Blockade. In 1987, Hartz Mountain acknowledged that 366 animal deaths and 2,700 known animal injuries as well as 56 human injuries had been blamed on Blockade. Hartz pulled it from the market, tested it on cats and kittens, and then reintroduced it with the *same ingredients!* The company *eventually* paid the Environmental Protection Agency $45,000 to settle charges that it failed to report animal illnesses and deaths from Blockade—a fat lot of good that did the animals harmed. Using too much of a product, using it too often, or using more than one product (such as a collar, dip, and powder) can cause a dangerous, even fatal, overdose. Long-term effects of flea pesticides include cancer, allergies, nerve damage, and other medical problems.

So, if you decide to use chemical warfare, be very cautious. Please, never hop off to work leaving your cat alone after a dip or shampoo. If you hear crying or see drooling, foaming at the mouth, body twitching, lethargy, diarrhea, difficulty breathing, difficulty moving, or vomiting, immediately call a poison control center for advice while driving to the veterinarian *with the product you used.*

Should you choose a chemical flea collar, be sure to hang it up somewhere for a few days before getting it anywhere near your cat. Then check for any allergic response, such as a rash around her neck, as there have been reports of adverse reactions.

Young cats and elderly cats are extra-susceptible to toxic reactions, but some healthy adult cats can suffer from them, too.

The Low-Toxicity Route

It surprises most people to know what every pesticide company tries to keep a secret: Pesticides are unnecessary, because washing with ordinary soap and water kills fleas! Soap penetrates the outer coating around fleas and destroys their natural defenses.

One nontoxic rinse that both kills fleas and soothes irritated skin can be made with a fresh lemon and hot water. Just slice the lemon thinly (including the peel), pour a pint of near-boiling water over it, and allow it to steep overnight. The next day, sponge the solution onto the animal's skin and let it dry or pour it into an empty spray bottle and use it as a spray (storing extra liquid in the refrigerator for a short time).

Bear in mind that citrus scents are offensive to some cats (they can be used to keep cats off furniture), so test your cat's tolerance before using them.

Gentle herbal shampoos can be quite effective and can be used as often as once a week, although too-frequent bathing can dry out your cat's skin. When shampooing, use warm water and begin with a ring of lather around the cat's neck so fleas cannot climb onto her face. You can also take the Darth Vader approach to flea control with the Flea Zapper. This battery-operated comb stuns and immobilizes fleas, using an extremely low electrical charge that most animals don't seem to mind or even feel. Conked-out fleas can be combed out of the hair and tidily sealed into one of the little baggies that comes with the comb. You can find it here: PETA.org/FleaZapper.

Homeopathic practitioners also have interesting advice on dealing with common problems such as fleas. Dr. Edgar Sheaffer, in *The Health Care Letter*, recommends combining a dietary approach, citrus dips, and remedies such as *Arsenicum album*, *lachesis*, *lycopodium*, or *Ledum palustre*. Another homeopathic veterinarian, Dr. George Macleod, believes a regular course of homeopathic sulfur, repeated after two-week intervals, may help make a cat less prone to flea infestations. These remedies may eliminate the fleas or reduce the cat's allergic reaction to them. If they don't, please try something else—don't simply live in hope.

A cat should look like a little person in a luxurious fur coat, not a tiny alligator. If your cat's skin is flaky and dry, it can be more attractive to fleas than healthy skin (fleas do not win *Better Homes &*

Gardens awards for how they like to live). Try adding fresh, raw foods such as sliced carrots and broccoli to your cat's food, and slip in a little evening primrose oil or flaxseed oil as well.

If you do want to use a pesticide, two of the least toxic natural pesticides are pyrethrins, derived from chrysanthemum flowers, and D-limonene, an extract from orange peel. Look for formulations that contain these active ingredients.

Many animal guardians add brewer's yeast (*not* nutritional yeast) to their cat's food: The theory is that the yeast gives the blood a slightly bitter odor that a tiny flea nose can detect and reject before actually taking a bite. You can get brewer's yeast for cats in tablet form, too. Another flea repellent is fresh garlic, crushed or ground, which is why there are no Italian flea circuses.

Flea Birth Control

Insect growth regulators (IGRs) offer an alternative to pesticides. Sold under brand names such as Ovitrol, Fleatrol, and Precor, IGRs contain insect hormones that disrupt the life cycle of the flea by preventing eggs and larvae from developing. They can be sprayed or used in room foggers and are available from some exterminators as well as from pet supply stores and catalogs.

There is a company called Fleabusters (1-800-666-3532) that uses a patented nontoxic sodium borate compound that it guarantees for up to one year. Several studies have shown the treatment to be highly effective. It also sells leabusters Rx for Fleas Plus and Fleabusters Flea Shampoo. See PETA.org/Fleabuster.

7
CAN TWO CATS BE TWICE AS NICE?

Who says so? Well, for starters, the cats sitting in the cages in every animal shelter in the world. Even for the snobs and recluses among them, sharing a home with another cat seems an infinitely more enjoyable proposition than no home at all. Not that I'm advocating cramming your house full of cats. I'm not. Things can go very wrong when a cat guardian becomes a cat hoarder and ends up overdoing it. Horror stories include respiratory viruses that spread and cannot be done away with when the number of cat lungs and noses gets out of control. But two cats make perfect sense, for you and for them.

If you love having one cat snuggled up to you, you'll adore having two. There are more subtle advantages as well. Anyone who has shared a bed with a cat knows that cats subscribe to the theory that too much uninterrupted sleep is bad for your health. When you have two cats and one stands on your windpipe in the middle of the night, demanding that you get up to play "where's the mouse?" they'll have each other. You can escort them both into the living room, close the door, and go back to bed.

Never fear that, were you to open your door and let one other cat walk through it, the current Ms. or Mr. Kitty wouldn't lavish as much attention on you. That's just nonsense—and selfish.

While two cats cannot live as cheaply as one (ask yourself, do your kids really need to go to college?), they do deliver twice as much affection. It makes sense. The more satisfied and happy your cat is, the less cranky and neurotic she will be. Cats are social beings, and as much as they love you, they are only "whole" when there's another cat around. Imagine if you lived with a gorilla. No matter how nice she was, you'd still want to talk to another human being once in a while. Ever see a lion living alone in the jungle? No, there's always a group of lions (OK, a pride), lollygagging around, their arms wrapped around each other, cleaning bits of congealed impala off each other's faces.

Truly well-adjusted cats seem to float along, inches off the carpet, exuding good vibrations, stopping only to rub up against your legs and purr down your neck. If you've got two of them doing this, the only thing you'll miss is earplugs.

The main worry is that your cat-in-residence will have an instant hissy-fit when the newcomer comes through the door. This is quite probable. Male cats have a reputation for being slightly more likely to fire up the Welcome Wagon than the womenfolk, unless the new cat is a male, but cats overall are not known for their magnanimity. However, even the most theatrical episodes of spitting jealousy can fade. Remember Moomin and Jarvis, the two devoted Siamese cats I mentioned in the introduction to this book? Although at first Jarvis would have bet the bank that he would never have wanted to share his life with Moomin, before long they became so devoted to each other that I'm sure he would have given his life for her.

WHERE TO GET KITTY NUMBER TWO

In this day and age, pet shop purchases are not only politically incorrect but out of the question. They create a market for cats at a time when humane societies are tearing their hair out over the companion animal overpopulation crisis. According to recent figures on such dismal matters, more than 27 million cats and kittens every year are unceremoniously booted through the front doors of animal shelters or abandoned in the countryside to starve to death while attempting to learn which berries to eat without a "how to" manual.

My recommendation is to be a model citizen. Rescue a cat or two (see above). Grant clemency to a cat or kitten who is likely becoming ever more disconsolate at your local shelter. Whatever you do, firmly resist the temptation to buy a "purebred" or "designer cat." Many have genetic problems resulting from their manipulation at human hands. Consider, for example, the Persian, bred for that pathetic Cabbage Patch Doll face that barely allows for normal breathing, or the Flame Point Siamese who, as a result of inbreeding to produce artificial colors at the tips (or points) of their tails, ears, and feet, suffers from weepy eyes. In my view, mongrels are the most! However, if you must have a Siamese or some other specific breed of cat, many shelters keep breed lists and work with breed rescue clubs. They are only too happy to match you up with the type of cat you fancy.

THE BASIC RULES

Whatever the origins of your new family member, whisk her directly to the veterinarian to have everything checked: gums (for anemia caused by hookworm), temperature (for feverish illness), red blood count (for feline leukemia), and on and on until your veterinarian can afford to buy a country estate. Oh, and make sure Kitty Number One is up to date on vaccinations before Kitty Number Two arrives.

Set aside a separate room in your home (not your bedroom, unless you want major tantrums from the ruling Ms. Puss) in which

TOP **TIP**

If you can, take *two* cats or kittens from the same family— two littermates, for example, or a mother and her son. There is extra security in having been together from the start, and there will be no problems with introductions.

to treat the newcomer for anything that ails her and to allow a couple of days of peace and quiet to get over the stress of travel and transfer.

Use as many bowls as you have cats. You aren't reenacting the Oliver Twist story wherein all the orphans have to grub for their morsels. With multiple bowls, one avoids unseemly spats, keeps the peace, and helps preserve everyone's dignity.

GETTING TO KNOW EACH OTHER

Introducing one cat to another can be stressful enough to make even an etiquette columnist swear out loud. Sure, some first encounters do go smoothly, but most cats look upon the arrival of Kitty Number Two in the same way a young maiden, waking up in the middle of the night to find teeth in her neck, views Dracula. Just remember that any inconvenience in the beginning will pale in comparison to the dose of double love that may last two decades. It's worth it. Trust me, and follow my advice.

Give Kitty Number Two enough room to escape the wrath of Kitty Number One. Provide Kitty Number Two with somewhere to hide—avoid staging the introduction in a small, unfurnished room. If you can observe unseen from outside, do. Second best, sit there and ignore them. Force yourself to ignore all the carryings-on (unless Kitty Number One is doing something truly life-threatening, like shoving Kitty Number Two out of a six-story window). If you can't look away, your "old" cat may put on a bigger show to try to win your apparently lost affections and to

TOP **TIP**

Make the initial intro after a big meal, when kitties are inclined to want to nap more than to fight. Patience is a virtue. Give them lots of time to make adjustments—sometimes it can take months for the relationship to gel.

impress you with how gallantly she can defend the household from this intruder.

If things get too tense, bring out the tinfoil balls, Cat Dancer, or other toys, preferably something on a string. If you start batting something about, you may lure one of the cats into the game, allowing them to forget their apprehensions about each other, let their guard down, and perhaps—one can dream—have fun. And give both cats a treat or two.

Whenever you see the opportunity, reassure Kitty Number One that she is still your absolute favorite by doing a lot of cooing and stroking and perhaps shoveling food in her direction. Remember always to keep the bowls far apart: Cats hate eating in front of strangers.

IF IT DOESN'T WORK OUT

Once in a while, two cats seem destined to despise each other unto death. If that happens or if for some other reason having another cat in the house is not going to work, it is imperative to take every precaution when looking for the next home for Kitty Number Two. Too many cats end up shuffled, like bags of laundry, from one place to another. This leads to trauma and confusion and produces unhappy and neurotic cats.

Be tough and discerning when interviewing prospective adopters. The words "I'll take that cat" definitely do not guarantee a good home. Hate me for saying this if you must, but it is far better to take Kitty Number Two to a well-run shelter (i.e., one that does not give animals to laboratories and has a sound adoption policy and sterilization requirements) than to pass her on to someone who thinks cats are cute but who hasn't thought through the lifetime commitment every cat requires and deserves. That means you will have to put on your inspector's cap, visit the prospective home yourself, check veterinary references, and ask questions. Again, *don't settle for anything less than the best, and check rather than trust,* because your temporary friend's life and lifetime happiness depend on it. For peace of mind, carefully consult *Guide to the Sale or Giveaway of a Dog or Cat,* free for downloadable from PETA here: PETA.org/FindingHome.

8
FOREVER FREE FROM PREGNANCY

Boys will be boys, but tomcats make boys look like angels. When your little "Tommy" becomes a real "Tom," which happens at about 10 months of age when his testicles descend, he will want to assert his sexual maturity in various ways.

When you wisely refuse to let him outside to get cauliflower ears from more experienced tomcats, he may have a pouty fit. In tomcats, pouty fits aren't events to look forward to. However, during such stressful times, your cat can't suppress his hormonally caused urges, so there is no point in your making a fuss, too. He will only resent you. Accept that he has become a man. Here is what you can expect, and this is what you can do:

One testosterone-induced, macho posturing behavior you can expect from an intact male cat is that he will back up to your furniture and spray urine all over it. His wild and free ancestors have marked their territory in this way since the dawn of time, their musky odor deterring invasion by other male cats anxious to settle down and start families. In most households, this does not go over well. Always remind yourself, however, that he didn't ask to be domesticated. We brought him indoors, so we get to clean up.

Some human males have a major problem even thinking about the minor surgery that will stop Tom from adding to (or wanting to add to) the feline overpopulation crisis. Just whisper the word "castration" and a ghastly pallor falls over many a man's face. The words "let's remove Tom's testicles" are apparently a direct assault on their own manhood.

During these times, it may be left up to a woman to show her strength. The surgery is simple, and while Tom will not retain his youthful soprano voice, he will stop caring about sex. Neutering prevents testicular cancer, too, for obvious reasons. It is also worth noting that, like the famous cartoon skunk Pepe LePew, male cats can detect the telltale scent of a female in heat miles away. Unlike Ulysses, however, they cannot plug their ears with wax and lash themselves to a ship's mast to avoid the sirens' call. You will have to do the humane version of that for them, and that means neutering.

As for girl cats, at about 5 to 6 months of age, their behavior can become so unsettling that it is easy to imagine that were they human, they would be experimenting with makeup and risking their ankle health in 4-inch stilettos.

Part of the secret cat plan to conquer the world must be for the females to be in heat almost nonstop and to go back into heat immediately after giving birth. No opportunity to reproduce is ever missed.

If your Ms. Kitty is in a breeding frame of mind, she may make weird noises that will help you understand how the word "caterwaul" originated. Female Siamese cats are in a class by themselves here. In moments of acute romantic need, they can outdo any horror movie "scream queen." It is a wonder any male gets within a football field of them.

Your cat may also contort herself into bizarre shapes that look as if someone dropped a flatiron on her back, and she may snap at you, literally, if you cannot or do not produce a handsome male prince to woo her.

During these times, your male cat will resent you in the deep and soulful way a human 16-year-old resents his parents for not letting him jump parked cars on a Harley Davidson. However, should you be tempted to let Kitty out or should you find yourself dialing a stud service, STOP. Don't touch that dial or that doorknob.

Temporary solutions do not solve lifetime, recurring problems. And if you let Thomas out, he is almost guaranteed to get ugly, painful, abscessed ears and other battle wounds, such as a scratched cornea or nose, that will require expensive veterinary attention. (Not to mention feline AIDS, for which there's no vaccine or cure!)

In Thomasina's case, her youthful disposition will be snatched away by endless numbers of litters of demanding kittens who will all need shots and whatnot and are very hard to place in this kitten-crowded world.

How's this for an amazing fact: If one female cat has a litter every six months (which is normal), each litter consisting of four kittens, half of whom are females who survive and breed, the original mother cat will be responsible for 36 cats in just 18 months. Well, you will be responsible for them if you didn't do what needs to be done.

Luckily, kitties can be made to forget the desires of the flesh. Thanks to sterilization, in the blink of an eye—or rather the snip of a pair of surgical scissors—your cat can become sensible and settled

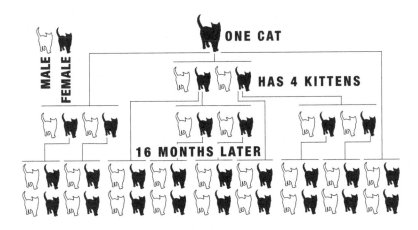

again. Your post-surgical puss will live happily ever after and devote all his or her love to ... you! While it is admittedly unnatural, so is eating food from a can, sleeping in a bed, and living with human beings.

There are other, not inconsequential, benefits to sterilization. Spayed cats' uteruses are removed during surgery, meaning that, thereafter, they cannot get uterine cancer. And studies show that even cats who only have their ovaries removed are less likely to get uterine cancer in their older years. Obviously, they also cannot get cancer of the ovaries without making it into *Ripley's Believe It or Not*.

Castrated males are less likely to get prostate cancer and, as mentioned earlier, cannot get testicular cancer.

WHEN TO DO THE DEED

You can have cats sterilized when they are mere tots: at 6 to 8 weeks of age. Or you can wait until sexual maturity, which comes at around 6 months for females and about 10 months for males. Some veterinarians prefer to wait, thinking it preferable to allow a cat to experience sexual maturity, but most do not think waiting makes any difference, and many warn against it.

Should you hold off, which I do not recommend, be careful. If your cat goes into heat, you will have to wait until the first break in her heat cycle, because most vets balk at spaying when the uterus is full of blood. Should Kitty have a sexual encounter, do not let that deter you from taking her to the vet as soon as she's out of heat. Don't let your cat have "just one litter." As one poster says, "Every Litter Hurts!"

GET THAT CAT OUT OF THERE!

Ever more veterinarians now realize that recovery from any surgery can be hampered by stress, such as the stress of being under the control of strangers in a strange environment. Conversely, nothing makes recovery smoother than being in a quiet, secure place, tended to by someone you love and trust. Home wins out over the animal hospital.

Always insist, if necessary, on collecting your cat as soon after surgery as is safe. Push! Avoid even one overnight stay, if you possibly can. If you work, try scheduling surgery for a Friday so that you can have the weekend with the patient. A two-day hospital stay is out of the question unless your cat needs elaborate medical care.

Should you worry about a medical emergency, have a cat carrier handy and make sure the car is gassed up in case you need to take the patient to an emergency hospital for attention. Comfort yourself with the knowledge that, had you left Kitty at the veterinarian's office where he was neutered, there would almost certainly not have been anyone on duty there overnight to notice any problem, let alone deal with it effectively. Usually only emergency animal hospitals have any overnight staff.

THE HOME RECOVERY CENTER

Set aside a very clean floor-level bed (topped with a clean cotton sheet) in a quiet room, and make sure your cat has no opportunity to pole vault herself onto tall cabinets or perform other activities that may separate the stitches. Your bedroom is probably ideal, as this is the most secure, comforting room in your home. I wouldn't recommend the bathroom, even if yours is cozy and warm. After a stressful experience, your cat wants to be with you, not alone. You'll also avoid the problem that a couple in Sweden had when they put their two cats in the bathroom and the cats turned on the shower and flooded the house.

Place fresh cat litter and fresh water close by. Monitor your feline patient to make sure she doesn't disturb the stitches by over-licking and that she starts drinking and eating enthusiastically after the anesthetic has worn off. Linger at the bedside to murmur reassuring words about liberation from the burdens of parenthood.

Over the next two weeks, seize opportune moments, as when

your cat has a leg pointed at the ceiling, to take discreet peeks to ensure that the surgical site hasn't become infected. If in doubt, call or visit the vet.

In years gone by, veterinary schools taught their students that animals were stoic and somehow didn't feel pain as we do. The same sort of ignorant thing used to be said of human infants and enslaved humans.

Such teaching has meant that a zillion cats have been left to suffer in pain from major surgery such as spaying. If your vet is from "the old school," they may not realize that times have changed and that the cat's central nervous system allows Precious to feel every bit as much pain as we do. Bring the vet up to date or consider a new vet.

Insist on painkillers. While fears of addiction used to stop doctors from prescribing medications, most vets have figured out how unlikely it is that your cat will end up robbing convenience stores to feed their drug habit. Most laypeople have enough common sense to realize that denying cats painkillers is bunk, but patients and patients' guardians still have a scary tendency to defer to authority, so it's good to listen to the vet's advice with your heart and your head. Put yourself in your cat's place. Would you want painkillers? If the answer is yes, demand them.

If Kitty is male, the surgery is minor. Although some swelling may cause him to walk like John Wayne for a few days, he should be fit as a fiddle almost immediately after he wakes up.

If Kitty is female, the surgery is major, so complete recovery will take seven to 10 days. After that, neither of you need ever look back (except to admire Kitty's derriere).

RESOURCES

Any veterinarian with an operating room is equipped to perform spay and neuter surgeries. But prices vary tremendously.

While some vets are too mean to help with the overpopulation crisis and will moan on about people in fancy cars driving their cat to a cheap spay surgery, others are kind souls who do their community a service by providing a low-cost incentive to sterilize. And some who could not care less about anything other than their business still realize they can acquire more long-term patients via this brief encounter!

If you are truly strapped for cash, see if your local humane society or SPCA operates a low-cost spay/neuter clinic or a program in cooperation with local veterinarians who reduce their fees.

Or try calling 1-800-248-7729 for SpayUSA, which gives referrals in over 1,900 low-cost sterilization programs and clinics nationwide. See PETA.org/SpayUSA.

9
TRAVEL TIPS TO KEEP KITTY SAFE

Barring a cataclysmic event, such as a meteorite about to collide with your house or your boss's announcement that you are being transferred to the lower Ganges basin, it is usually a bad idea to contemplate moving your cat any greater distance than from the chair to the couch.

Out of 1,000 cats, 999 (possibly more) loathe getting into a car, let alone having the car move out of the driveway, and most will hate you long after hell has frozen over if you have the audacity to buy them an airline ticket. Birds fly, not cats. (In the U.S., trains stopped taking cats and other animals in the 1980s for reasons not even Amtrak or the people at *Trains* magazine remember.) Just in case that changes, always check with the train company.

All that said, if you tread very carefully, it is possible to manage Kitty's travel plans well enough to emerge smelling like catnip.

MUST YOU DO THIS AT ALL?

This is the million-dollar question. Obviously, if you are a sensible person who has to move, your cat is part of your family and you will not be casting about for new "parents" for your kitty. That is only an option if you think of a cat as a replaceable, insentient object, like yard-sale bric-a-brac, and readers of this book do not think of cats in that way.

Do you have to go to wherever it is that you are thinking of going? I am quite serious. If the answer is yes and the trip is a relatively quick out-and-back one, perhaps the solution is not to pack Kitty's valise but to let her wait, safe at home, for your return.

"Safe at home" does not mean being holed up at the veterinarian's. Only sadists would think of leaving a child in a cage in a hospital, exposed to diseases and the cries of others in distress, and the same goes for Kitty. Nor is an institution, e.g., a cattery, a fun place to be when your folks are out of town. "Safe at home" means finding the right cat-sitter.

BE PICKY ABOUT PICKING A CAT SITTER

It's hard to get good help these days. It probably always was. Cat sitting is not something to entrust to the kid down the block who seems really nice or to some entrepreneur who happened to find enough loose change under the cushions on the couch to run an ad. Cat sitters must be chosen with as much care as a French chef chooses vegetables (but without the squeezing).

Your best bet is to select someone you know personally, such as your sister or mother, providing this person (a) is sane, (b) doesn't bear a grudge against you, and (c) demonstrably likes and understands cats.

Coworkers only enter the running if you have been to their homes and like how they interact with their own cat(s). The home visit is necessary, because your colleagues might be geniuses at, say, accounting and seem charming at the water cooler but could still let Tiddles out the screen door on day one, assume the cat will come home, and not summon you off the beach. Goodbye forever, Tiddles.

Let us consider the outside sitter. I don't say "professional" sitter, because sitter services are not usually regulated or bonded (not that such pacifiers would amount to much). Sadly, there is usually no knowing if sitters are truly experienced, trained, and perceptive or if they can actually differentiate between a cat in the pink of health and one with the heaves. This is not to say that there aren't great sitters out there, but placing your trust in the innate goodness of humankind is not an appropriate approach when leaving your cat's life in unfamiliar hands. Be a stickler.

If you must use an outside sitter, here are some basic rules to follow:

1 **A big smile is not a reliable reference.** Check references carefully. (Try to determine if the folks providing the glowing endorsements are actually the sitter's relatives and friends.)

2 **Google the sitter.** Then call the Better Business Bureau, your local chamber of commerce, and any and all animal protection organizations within 30 miles to ask if they have ever had a complaint about this person.

3 **Meet the sitter in advance and ask leading questions about cats and their care.** (Wrong answers? Wrong sitter.)

4 **Sign a contract**—but not one that exempts the sitter from liability in the case of kitty illness, accident, or death.

5 **Make sure the sitter agrees to check in with you every day,** no matter where you are.

6 **Leave your contact information,** including a phone number, as well as contact information for your best cat-aware friend or relative and that of your vet on the sitter's cell phone and taped to your fridge in case she loses her phone.

7 **Leave water in bowls in many rooms of the house.** (If the sitter is struck by lightning, causing your house key to melt, Kitty is in far greater danger of dying of dehydration than of starving to death.)

8 **Have someone you know and who knows cats check on the cat** at least every two days.

9 **Worry!** This can help you think of other precautions.

THE *ONLY* WAY TO FLY

Charles A. Lindbergh was once asked why he had not taken his beloved kitten, Patsy, along to keep him company on his 1927 historic transatlantic flight. He answered, "It's too dangerous a journey to risk a cat's life."

Since cats don't have wings, there is only one right way to fly a cat.

Reuben, a dearly loved young tomcat, learned this lesson the hard way when his people popped him into a plastic carrier, handed him over the counter to reassuring airline officials, and walked trustingly out of the airport. Reuben found himself on a conveyor belt bound for the belly of a jumbo jet parked at the gate on a far-away continent. Although the tag on his cage read, "DESTINATION: USA," he never made it. To this day, no one knows—or is telling—what became of Reuben.

Regrettably, Reuben's story is not even close to unique. Cats and dogs sent as cargo commonly arrive injured, traumatized, or dead—or never arrive at all. They suffer from heatstroke or freeze when heating or cooling systems fail, and fail they do. They are crushed when cargo shifts during turbulence and are even run over by baggage conveyors. And there is no one to console them when the airbus behaves like a ski jumper during heavy turbulence.

What is unusual is the story of Tabitha, a tabby cat who was lost aboard a Tower Airlines 747 flight from Los Angeles to New York. PETA was contacted to help rescue her.

Somehow, Tabitha had escaped from her carrier, another frequent cause of missing cats. Perhaps the latch was faulty or a traumatized Tabitha managed to find a way to squeeze out. Although the disappearance could have taken place during loading or unloading, a psychic called in by Tabitha's family didn't think so. She had a vision of Tabitha squashed up inside the metal paneling in the plane's cargo hold. She believed that Tabitha was staying alive by licking drops of water that had condensed from a pipe inside the cargo bay wall.

Airline officials, knowing their company would lose hundreds of thousands of dollars if they grounded the 747 for a thorough search, refused to do so.

It took 12 agonizing days before PETA and attorney Donald David managed to come close enough to getting a court order against the airline to persuade company executives to let a search party onto the plane.

Meanwhile, the plane had been in the air between San Juan, Miami, New York, and Los Angeles many times, logging over 32,000 miles! Jimmy the Greek would have given a thousand to one odds on finding Tabitha alive.

Within seconds of the psychic's entering the cargo bay, she pointed to the exact spot where Tabitha was hidden—frightened and thin but alive!

Tabitha's airline horror story is the one in a million with a happy ending. Tabitha's owner, Carol Ann Timmel, is so happy that she has written a children's picture book about the saga, called *Tabitha: The Fabulous Flying Feline* (Walker & Co.). The book can be found on AmazonSmile.com.

On a more down-to-earth note, no cash settlement can replace a treasured family member, but in the case of animals hurt, killed, or "misplaced" during flight, families are never awarded damages of any significance: The courts have ruled that the animals' lives are worth less than the value of a Samsonite suitcase.

TOP **TIP**

If you have to take Tiger on the road, in case of an emergency or an accident, for example, take along his health records. To help him feel more at home and adjust more quickly, include his toys and bedding in your luggage, too.

In fact, the way some animals are thrown about and otherwise abused by airline companies, they might as well be the luggage you see dropped out of the plane in those endurance test ads.

Imagine the agony of the people who had animals aboard a jet that crashed in Denver some years back. Humane officers couldn't persuade, cajole, or bully airport or carrier officials to let them inside the hold to rescue animals trapped in the cargo section of the wreckage until days after the crash!

One last point: According to retired Federal Aviation Association officer Jim Wippert, all commercial aircraft cargo holds must have a fire-extinguishing system in the cargo hold. Because these systems are expensive and heavy and require continuous maintenance, most aircraft manufacturers prefer to use the limited-airflow method. The theory behind limiting air flow is that a fire would soon use up all the oxygen in the hold and extinguish itself.

In other words, the amount of air going into a hold is limited by design. An animal in the hold has a limited amount of oxygen to breathe. When the oxygen is gone, so are the animals. It happens. The airlines don't like to talk about it, and most airline personnel are not aware of this design requirement.

The moral of the Tabitha and Reuben stories is this: The only way to fly a cat is inside the cabin, with you or someone you trust. All the tea in China couldn't make up for the loss of your cat, so even if you have to take out a loan to fly another human along, do it or you may hate yourself forever and be justified in doing so.

Most airlines allow at least one animal per cabin, some no more than one, so book well in advance. For international flights, a government-certified health certificate is required for reentry into the U.S. and you will need to check for quarantine restrictions, which vary from country to country.

For travel within the U.S., all that is usually required is a certificate from your veterinarian showing that your cat has a current rabies vaccination, but always double-check with the airline and the state health department to avoid surprises on the big day.

Regulation cat flight carriers made of sturdy, heavy, crush-resistant plastic are available at pet supply stores and from the airlines. They fit perfectly under the seat in front of you. During the flight, although you should never open the carrier door for fear of an escape, you can reassure Kitty that the ugly sound of that jet engine and those horrible bumps are really hundreds of little mice feet beating on the floor as the mice run away, whispering, "Ooooh, a cat!"

Here are some other do's and don'ts:

- Always try your hardest to book a nonstop flight. Transfers just add hazard potential.
- Don't fly during extremely hot or cold weather if you can avoid it; in summer, choose cooler nighttime flights.
- Even if your cat is high-strung, it is not recommended (by the International Air Transport Association, the American Veterinary Medical Association, or me) to administer a tranquilizer. If Kitty gets woozy or conks out, she could drift off face-down with her nose buried in the traveling towel. There is the danger of suffocation. Read the International Air Transport Association's warning message here: PETA.org/LiveCargoWarning. There is, however, a pheromone-based melatonin "calming spray" that might help: PETA.org/CalmingSpray. And don't forget the Bach flower remedies listed elsewhere in this book.
- Do not feed or give water one hour or less before flight time. Try to time feeding and drinking so that your cat has done both and urinated *and* defecated before boarding (you may be able to place a tiny foil litter tray in the carrier).
- Never leave the carrier unattended for even a moment. It's a crazy world, and even babies get stolen from hospital cribs.
- Always make sure that both cat and cat carrier are very clearly

marked with your name and all your contact information.
It never hurts to add the words "REWARD IF FOUND."
Motives are unimportant when you and kitty are desperate
to find each other.

GETTING KITTY INTO THE CARRIER

Sounds simple, doesn't it! It is, if Kitty is comatose, is used to sleeping
in the carrier, or often finds a cache of favorite treats hidden inside
it. But if Kitty is halfway functional and only used to going to the
vet in that thing, getting her into it without losing claw-size parts of
your shoulder is as simple as making something edible out of garden
mulch. You will have to call on your powers of persuasion and,
possibly, guile.

Because cats can see and hear, don't parade about with the carrier
in hand or get it noisily out of the closet. Subtlety and speed are
called for. Plan your maneuver carefully. And don't smile too much.
The cat's no fool. Try to act as if nothing's up.

Here are the steps to take:

1 **Make sure the carrier floor is comfy,** not lumpy, barren, cold
(don't store it in the wine cave), or lined with thin paper. A warm
towel makes a good floor covering. And put a treat in at the back.

2 **Make sure the door works well and closes tightly.** If necessary,
oil the hinges. There may be a time and place for fumbling, but,
as on a date, this isn't it.

3 **Try to get the carrier as near as possible to the cat, ever so
quietly, without letting the cat see it.** This means that once you
pick the cat up, there won't be far to go. Keep the carrier at chest level
(yours) so that you don't have to bend down at a crucial moment.

4 **Pick Tiddles up, facing away from the carrier** and, talking gently
to her so that she will never trust you again, move backward if
necessary, until you are just in front of the carrier.

5 Back her into the carrier, gently but firmly. Before you let go, keep one hand inside the carrier at her face level to stop her from dashing out as energetically as she would if given a clear view of the escape hatch.

6 Latch the door. Cover the carrier with a lightweight towel, making sure Kitty can breathe. Pick the carrier up evenly. (Some people seem to forget that there's a cat onboard and start swinging it about, banging it into doors, holding it at weird angles, and otherwise misbehaving.)

7 Depart. Do not be tempted, for any reason, to open the carrier until it's safe to do so (when you are shut in a room somewhere).

There. That was easy, wasn't it?

GETTING KITTY INTO THE CAR

Dogs may drool out the window, bark at bicyclists, and snort the air as it rushes past, but they are not cats. Cats regard even slow-moving vehicles in much the same way claustrophobics view closets. If you multiply by 6 million that teeny bit of skepticism you once entertained about the structural integrity of an old bridge or how well your car would fare if you accidentally flipped it over, you will have some idea of how comfortable most cats are with motorized transport. Even the horn scares and disgusts them.

A lot of this is probably attributable to the fact that the only time most cats see the inside of a car is when their next sight will be the inside of a veterinarian's office. Cars mean something unpleasant is getting ever closer.

Some cats are introduced to car rides for pure fun in their kittenhood and actually seem to enjoy them. Once in a blue moon, you see some showoff driving along with a cat draped over his shoulder. This does not alter the fact that cats and cars are a bad mix.

For example, if a vehicle backfires, a gun-shy dog may cower but a cat will flee (and in strange territory, chances of recovery are slim). George, one of the most dearly loved cats ever to grace a household, was lost in this way.

George was en route to the vet when it happened. As he was lifted out of the car and into his "dad's" arms, a trash truck turned on the grinder. George must have thought a monster was about to snatch him into its jaws. He fled for his life, leaving deep claw marks in the arms of the man who tried to stop his escape. Ads in the paper, cards left on veterinarians' bulletin boards, enquiries—all came to naught.

Whatever became of George we do not know.

Cars also have windows and seats. While it may be impossible for a wolfhound or even a corgi to clamber out through a tiny crack in the window that lets the driver pay a gas station attendant or a toll, most cats are like octopuses and can squeeze their way out of an opening the size of one in a toothpaste tube. As for seats, I have never heard of a dog getting caught in the springs under a seat or having to be cut out of the metalwork over the wheelbase, but both things frequently happen to cats. Extricating them wastes a chunk of a person's life and sometimes takes a chunk out of the car. The cat may emerge physically intact but could suffer emotional scars that never heal.

If you are going to put a tiger in your Toyota, here's how to do it right:

1 *Always* use a sturdy carrier. Double-check that the carrier door is absolutely secure. Never let your cat loose in the car. Cat guardian Alison Green says, "If, for any reason, you find yourself in a car with an unrestrained cat, don't ever, ever, ever open the door or window until you have the situation completely under control. Countless cats have been lost at tollbooths and rest stops this way."

2 Keep the carrier from wobbling by creating as flat a surface as possible for it to sit on. (Pack a towel around the outside of the

carrier, once situated, if you need to.) Do not let Tiddles see that she is headed for the car. Drape a breathable cloth over the carrier before heading out the door, place the carrier on the flat surface in the car, then rearrange the cloth so that she can see you, if possible, but not out any window. The sight of the earth or sky speeding past causes most cats to panic, begin open-mouthed breathing, howl miserably, and contemplate suicide at the stoplight.

3 **Pad the inside of the carrier with something comfy**, like a towel, to make travel easier by softening bumps.

4 **Play the radio softly to drown out traffic noises.** (Try a soothing classical music station.)

5 **Talk to your cat as you go.** If she complains, always answer reassuringly. (Here's an actual, sample conversation. Comment: "Meow!!!" Response, "It's all right. I know." Question: "Meooooow?!" Response, "Yes, Sweetie, I know. It's OK.")

6 **Remember how frightened you were when you got into the car with your nearsighted oldest relative, now retired to Florida, at the wheel?** Don't drive like that. Avoid lurching forward, brake smoothly, and imagine you are delivering crystal glassware that will shatter if you do not look ahead and steer clear of sewer covers.

7 **When you arrive at your destination, let Kitty scope out the new indoor setting from the sanctity of her carrier,** then offer her food, water, and litter outside it. In strange surroundings, ensure that all doors and windows are shut as tightly as can be before even one whisker emerges from that carrier.

ROOM AT THE INN?

Although almost every guesthouse, hotel, and motel in the world allows even the most ill-mannered human child through its portals without so much as a peep, someone with an absolutely impeccably behaved cat can find the door slammed in her face.

However, there are a number of hotels and resorts that score extra points for being cat-friendly.

Hotel/motel chains that allow animals include Holiday Inn, Best Western, La Quinta, Red Roof Inn, Comfort Inn, Motel 6, and Super 8. Four Seasons Hotels allow animals worldwide. Some restrictions apply and vary from hotel to hotel. Call 1-800-332-3442 for information about a specific hotel. Other animal-loving and classy accommodations include New York's Hotel Pierre and Los Angeles' Hotel Bel-Air.

10

HELP! MY CAT HAS DISAPPEARED

This chapter could save your cat's life.

One way not to lose things would be to thread a string through every single object you own. When something goes missing, all you have to do is follow the string. Sadly, this doesn't work for non-things, like cats. If it did, this chapter would not so bluntly proclaim the horror of a missing cat.

Although there are few deeds that beat rescuing someone from danger for securing their undying love, admiration, and even hero-worship, there are easier ways to curry favor. If your cat disappears, you will have to earn your detective degree and hero status on the super-fast track. It's no good trusting that your cat will be like miraculous Camila, a cat who found her way home by walking 125 miles through Portugal. Something untoward can easily happen. Every minute counts, or Kitty could end up somewhere decidedly unsavory—upside down on a laboratory table "advancing the cause of science" or flat as a pancake on the freeway.

Of course, as with most ordeals, an ounce of prevention is worth a pound of cure, especially since some conditions, such as rigor mortis, are incurable.

This means keeping tabs on Kitty from the moment you make him your own, always securing doors and windows and only letting your cat out with a chaperone or in a secure enclosure, such as a modified IKEA bookcase.

It means being wary of messengers, visitors, children, and other careless souls who don't realize that a vigilant feline can slip out through a crack in a screen door and could get as far as the Yukon by nightfall. (Read "New York" if you actually live in the Yukon.)

It means taking a set of good pictures of Kitty now, just in case, and making sure Kitty is always well dressed, i.e., wearing a clearly legible, current tag. The collar must be detachable to prevent your cat from hanging himself (it happens) and immediately replaced should it vanish. Consider buying in bulk.

Kitty should also be microchipped and the information kept up to date. If you are in the military, too young to be settled, or contemplating divorce or if you have nomadic tendencies, always make sure the information to track you down is current. Set yourself a calendar reminder. Ask your vet where to get this simple injection for your cat, or call Merck and Co. at 1-800-444-2080. The company markets systems called AVID and Home Again. Just don't use it as the sole ID method.

Don't think for a moment that your cat can't or won't leave home, given half a chance. It's not that a cat wants to walk away forever; it's just that even a harmless little stroll can turn into a lifetime loss. Snow and rain can mask or obliterate the vital scents that would lead Kitty home. An interesting excursion into a drain or culvert can become a nightmare when a sudden surge of water blocks the escape route. Accidents happen. And as clever as cats are, even they are no match for foul play.

Some members of our own species called "bunchers" make a living from setting traps for cats or even netting them straight off the street for resale to laboratories. Years ago, the prestigious Mayo Clinic in Minnesota was found harboring seven of 13 dearly loved animal companions who had all been stolen from homes in a nearby county.

Cats are used for everything from live training tools for pit bulls to shark bait in Hawaii. In England, Russia, and even South Dakota, cat fur has been found used as trim on coats. It is imported from Asia under various other names and made into fur trim, glove lining, and even cat toys!

And, yes, Virginia, there truly are wannabe satanic cults, sometimes composed of teenagers who derive desperately sought feelings of power from torturing cats. In Florida, whole blocks of cats have disappeared around All Hallows Eve, or Halloween. In Sacramento, the organs and entrails of cats have been found arranged in symbolic ways on people's lawns.

Finally, there are few things worse than never knowing what became of someone you love, not knowing whether they are dead or alive (and if they died, how).

So, always keep the apple of your eye well in view, safe at home with you, and then you can use this chapter to line Kitty's litter box.

MOOMIN'S TALE

I lost Moomin, the little Siamese kitten I described in the introduction to this book, when she was in her middle years. It happened because of my carelessness.

It was summer, peak theft season. I had a reception to attend, my air conditioning was broken, and it was hot. I left my bedroom window open just a few inches, trying to capture the breeze and push some of that muggy Washington air out the same way it had come in.

When I got back to the house that night, Moomin was nowhere to be found. I called and called and walked the yard with a flashlight. Nothing.

The next morning, my panic rising, I combed the bushes, searched neighbors' yards, and talked to the mail carrier but had no luck. By nightfall, I was beside myself with worry.

I did everything you will find listed in this chapter, and I did it all twice. By the 10th day, I felt as if my heart had been crushed by a steamroller. Where was she? Was she alive or dead? How could I have allowed something to happen to such a vulnerable little cat?

After nine days of frantic searching, a friend suggested I call a psychic. I thought the idea was absurd, but at that point I would have tied oranges to my ears if someone had suggested it might bring Moomin home.

I reached the psychic by phone all the way across the country. She told me not to recount any circumstances surrounding the disappearance but to express my feelings and to describe my beloved cat. That was tough. Tears streamed down my cheeks and my voice broke up as I traced Moomin's face in my mind and said how much I loved her.

At some point, the psychic said, "Let me tell you what happened." I set aside every thread of skepticism to listen.

Moomin, she said, had "left through a window when it was dark, walked down a few steps, and crossed a very big road directly outside your house. It was very quiet and she felt adventurous, so she started to explore in a field on the other side of the road.

"When it started to rain, she hid under some bushes. Later, the rain stopped. She returned to the road, but by this time, it was light and everything had changed. The road was full of cars. Moomin was too frightened to cross back. She heard you calling, but she couldn't come to you."

I was stunned. Moomin *had* left by the window. There is a small set of steps near it. Outside my house there was a six-lane highway— a commuter route that was quiet at night but chock-full of traffic by morning. It *had* rained in the early hours of that morning 10 days earlier.

The psychic was in California. I was calling from Maryland. I had no idea what to make of this, but I kept quiet and listened to what she had to say.

"Moomin is tired and scared," she continued, "but she's still alive." The psychic believed my little cat was across the road, living under a house, eating out of bowls of food left for other cats. She wished me luck and refused payment.

I was out of the house and across the road in a flash, walking among the houses, calling and calling until dark. Again, nothing. It had all been rubbish. Moomin was nowhere to be found. What more could I do? I was desolate.

The next day, the phone rang. The caller had seen one of my big plyboard signs at a nearby intersection.

"I've been trying to decide whether to call or not," she said. "I think your cat is living under my porch, eating out of my cat's dish. I've been thinking of keeping her."

The caller lived almost a mile away, straight through the field on the other side of my street.

Moomin lay on my bed that night while I sat watching her, feeling as happy as can be. She was very thin, very dirty, extremely hungry, and totally exhausted. She had gulped the food I gave her, then, most uncharacteristically, fallen asleep without cleaning herself. For the first time in her life, her ears twitched at every sound and she woke many times until I assured her that her return was not merely a dream.

I imagined how frightened she must have been, seeking refuge under that house every night, living on scraps. She would have been startled by raccoons and opossums and wouldn't have known which humans were friend, which ones foe. How she must have longed for her home and hoped for those she loved to come and rescue her.

I knew how lucky we both had been. How close I had come to losing her forever, psychic or no psychic. I knew I would never be so foolish as to let Moomin or any other cat out of my sight again.

A STEP-BY-STEP RECOVERY PLAN

If Kitty goes on the lam, you will need to move like the wind, by which I certainly do not mean whirl about quickly and purposelessly. Luck is great and timing is important, but organization is everything.

Here Are the Basic Rules:

1 No matter what your commitments may be at work, they must wait. The material world isn't as important as your cat's life. Recruit relatives to look after the kids. Tear up your dance card. Postpone your wedding. Take emergency leave. Do whatever it takes to free yourself up to find your cat.

2 Make absolutely sure that the number you are about to plaster up everywhere is always answered, that no call or text is missed. If you post your e-mail, check your spam folder.

No matter who else you are expecting to hear from, no one is more important than the person who has found your cat or has a lead to his whereabouts. Record a new phone message along these lines: "Please don't hang up if you have information about my missing cat. I must speak to you. If you can leave your name and number, please do so, twice, speaking very clearly. If you do not have a number, this phone should be answered by a live person between x and y today, or you can reach [someone else you absolutely trust] at [another number you are absolutely sure of]. Your call is vital to me. If I do not call you back, it means your number didn't record clearly. Please let me talk to you. Thank you."

3 Find out which humane societies and animal control agencies exist in your area. Don't assume there are only one or two. Ask each place you call, "Where else should I check?" Then ask again, and ask every time you call. Different people give you different leads. Check online, ask veterinary hospital receptionists, and call pet shops and anyone else who might have a clue.

4 Visit each shelter every day, no matter how often they assure you that they will call you if Kitty shows up. Lots of called-in and turned-in animals go unrecognized or ignored at busy shelters. Trust me on this.

Ask to see the Lost and Found book. Be pleasant but persistent. You need these people, but very quietly in your own head, assume they are at worst incompetent or at best too busy to be relied upon. I love most shelter workers, and if your cat's life is on the line, you will need help from them—but saving your cat's life means never relying completely on anyone other than yourself, particularly overworked people who see dozens of cats a day.

5 Make clear copies of the best photo of your cat you can find. Ask that a copy be glued or taped into the Lost Book in every shelter, and put one on every bulletin board, including in grocery stores and veterinary offices. Post it on your neighborhood internet sites, on any local meet-up group sites, and anywhere you can think of.

6 Don't discount the newspapers. Run an ad. Say only, "Lost cat. [Color]. Reward. [Phone number]." Don't mention Kitty's gender or breed (if any), hair coat length, or any other confusing details. Most people couldn't sex an elephant accurately, let alone a cat, and their idea of breeds would make a show judge weep. You won't want to miss that all-important call because Mr. Finder thinks your calico girl is a neutered Himalayan boy. If necessary, keep running the ad until the paper goes out of business. Check the Found and the Lost ads in the paper daily. People at newspapers sometimes mix the ads up.

7 Don't chintz on the reward. How much could you rustle up if you needed emergency surgery or if your roof sprang a leak? You are not tipping a server, you are trying to lure people who otherwise would not give a hoot or put a minute into finding your irreplaceable angel. Cough up.

8 Try to get local radio and television stations to run an announcement for you. If there is something notable about your cat that might engage their interest, mention it. For example, note if your infant child hasn't been able to sleep since Kitty's been missing or if your cat has just arrived from Minnesota and may be trying to hoof it back there—anything quirky or endearing might win him a life-and-death mention.

9 Strip-search the neighborhood:
   - Talk to mail carriers, delivery people, and folks you haven't uttered a word to or wanted to in years. Knock on doors. Show the picture.
   - Bribe children—they hear and see more than adults do.
   - Use a flashlight to peer into drains, parked cars, and sheds.
   - Go out at night and call your cat's name when all is quiet. Listen carefully for the faint "meow" of a cat stuck backward down a standpipe. For the first time in your life, you'll find yourself wishing cats barked. Don't forget that cats can get stuck inside small spaces in walls and vehicles and can't extricate themselves.

10 Salvage or buy some giant pieces of plywood. Spray paint your simple, standard message on them:

BIG REWARD

LOST CAT

[COLOR]

[RELIABLE CONTACT NUMBER]

11 Put flyers in vets' offices in case your cat has been injured or has taken ill. Drop them into storm doors in the area, and put posters on telephone poles. Cover a large radius. Many cats are found 1 to 2 miles away.

12 It's useful to register with the Lost and Found Pets database at PETA.org/LostFoundPets. And although you have lost a cat, there's no harm in signing up for PETA.org/FindToto and PETA.org/LostMyDoggie to have your neighbors alerted by phone. Also, PETA.org/DogsFindingDogs will try to track a dog by scent, so it should be able to do the same for a cat. The company works only in D.C., Delaware, Maryland, Pennsylvania, and Virginia but has a nationwide network.

13 You have the legal right to visit laboratories and dealers to look for your feline friend. Contact them quickly!

14 Follow any and all leads, and do anything anyone suggests. Consult a psychic, and light a candle for Saint Jude if you feel like it. Who knows what will bring Kitty home?

Most importantly, never, ever give up. Look everywhere and keep looking. Cats have been found locked inside a soda machine recently serviced by a mechanic, trapped inside the wheel of a private jet, and even inside a Mercedes shipped by sea in a crate nailed shut and bound for Europe. I once united a family with their dog, Blossom, after five months. Their daughter had raised Blossom from puppyhood, then dropped her off at her parents' home while she moved across the country. She didn't speak "dog" well enough to be able to explain to Blossom what was going on, and the pup didn't understand. Seizing an open-door opportunity one morning, Blossom set off to reunite herself with the daughter. Who knows what happened, but when I found her, Blossom was living like a tramp, holed up in a culvert along an interstate. Her coat was full of sticks and clumps of dirt, and she had been grazed by a car.

Whether the daughter ever realized how she had let Blossom down, I have no idea. But I do know how pleased the parents were to see Blossom and how delighted she was to see them again.

One final word: The Incredible Journey is not something you can count on. Few cats or other animals prevail when trying to trek their way home over long distances. It happens—even over thousands of miles—but the odds are stacked against mere cats in this harsh, mechanized, auto-filled world.

11
DECIPHERING CAT COMMUNICATION

Human beings can be such supremacists! For decades, scientists solemnly gave lectures in which they declared that what separates "man from beast" is that only humans use language. After a while, sensible people started giving the scientists some well-deserved raised eyebrows. According to a study conducted by Alan Beck, 99% of guardians report talking to the animals they live with and 75% of children say they confide in the animals they love.

It's not a one-way street. The fact is that most—perhaps all—animals use some form of language, even if we can't understand or recognize it as such. Elephants, for example, communicate at frequencies too low for us to hear. Ethologists eavesdropping on elephants in the African bush used to pick up strange low rumbling sounds on their sophisticated microphones and think the pachyderms' stomachs were rumbling because they were peckish. Eventually they put two and two together.

As for cats, they can hear sounds at frequencies of 65,000 cycles per second or more, which is incredibly inconvenient for mice, who commonly squeak at that frequency. Cats can also hear sounds more than two octaves higher than the highest note humans can hear without instrumentation.

Behaviorists (clearly a group with too much time on their hands and someone else footing the bill) have learned that birds speak different dialects, depending on the region in which they grow up. Observers taped the sounds of crows in the south of France and played them back to crows in northern France. The crows in the north went, "Huh?" They hadn't a clue what the other crows were cawing about. Of course, in the wine regions, perhaps none of the crows can understand what the others are saying after a few beakfuls of delicious champagne grapes.

Chimpanzees cannot make human sounds, because their vocal cords aren't constructed in the same way ours are, but they readily learn American Sign Language and even make up their own words. One chimpanzee, called Washoe, signed "water" and "fruit" when she tasted her first watermelon. When she didn't like something her keeper did, she swore at him, signing, "You dirty toilet."

The list of interspecies communications we have managed to figure out is long. For example, marine biologists believe that whales actually sing their histories as human tribal peoples do, passing information down through the generations, each year changing part of their elaborate song to mark new events.

We know that tiny prairie dogs have a vast repertoire of language. They not only warn each other of pending intrusion but also can use different sounds to convey what species the intruder belongs to, whether he or she is familiar, and what the intruder's intentions seem to be. Prairie dogs even use adjectives! Their language apparently goes something like this: One prairie dog says to another, "There's that skinny fella from Prudential again. He's got a trainee with him. Get in your burrows or they'll try to sell you insurance."

Many scientists who study cetaceans (whales and dolphins) believe our language studies have failed because these big-brained beings "talk" too fast for us to keep up, their signals are too sophisticated for us to interpret, and dolphins may communicate in whole pictures, much as we receive television transmissions.

As if that weren't weird enough, consider this: Even that fly on the wall may be telling other flies what he's seen. The human ear can only differentiate gaps between a hundred words a minute. More than that sounds like ... a buzz!

The communication patterns of bees are legendary, and their dances are highly detailed and purposeful.

If all the other reasons to forgo dissection in school weren't enough, frogs communicate by sending vibrations through leaves and clicking out messages with their toes, similar to Morse code.

It's a wonderful world. But back to cats ...

WHAT WE HAVE HERE IS A FAILURE TO COMMUNICATE

Since we're not smart enough to learn "cat," cats have been stuck with having to find ways to communicate with us. Some are less than satisfactory. Take Lisa Lange's cat, Camila, who sticks a claw up Lisa's nostril every morning to let her know it's breakfast time.

Most cats have more important things to do than teach us how to purr fluently, so how can we break the language barrier?

First, the don'ts.

Someone once said, "If I tell my dog, 'Come here,' he runs right over with a 'Yes, what can I do for you?' look. The cat's response is 'Put it in writing and I may get back to you.'"

Some people let the creepy old word "master" go to their heads. They believe that the way to communicate with another animal is by giving orders. You've seen certain people with their dogs. All they seem to do is issue commands. It's "Sit, Max," "Here, Max," "Be quiet, Max," "Max, down. I said 'Down!' Max," "Heel!" "No!" "Come." Their dogs must lie awake nights wondering who signed them up for the Marine Corps. What a life!

Other people whine in a high-pitched voice, as if their animals were demented. "Ooooh, the itty bitty goopie schmoopie!" Even Attila the Hun probably appreciated a bit of baby talk once in a while, and being schmaltzed beats being bossed about, but cats have dignity and presence. That glint in their eye probably means, "If you don't stop that, I'm going to give you back my breakfast!" Which reminds me that PETA carries a whimsical "Warning: Cat Vomit" floor sign, available at PETA.org/Store.

If you must let your cat know that some behavior or other displeases you, try a little hiss—that's what their mom would do. You may also spit (or use a spitting surrogate, such as a plant mister) gently if the situation gets out of hand. If the bad behavior is a bite or a scratch, the most effective way to show your displeasure is to walk away immediately and without a word. Cutting off playtime or petting sends a very clear message. Never throw anything, strike the animal, use your hand to discipline them, or make a very loud noise—or you may create lifetime loathing.

Hopeless optimists try to read human words into cat sounds. I was in someone's living room once when she grabbed me by the arm, pointed to her cat, who had just very distinctly said, "Meow," and whispered, "Did you hear that? She said, 'Mama!'" There was nothing to do but nod energetically, then suddenly remember that I had left the oven on at home. Wishful interpretations can prevent us from accepting that cats simply don't care to learn our language. They have a perfectly good one of their own. Just because Berlitz or Rosetta Stone hasn't marketed the six-week course in it doesn't mean we can't learn to speak "cat."

THE EYES HAVE IT

It's lucky we're dealing with cats, not cuttlefish. Cuttlefish, or squid, are amazing, complex invertebrates who communicate by flashing waves, blotches, and circles of ever-changing color over their bodies. To touch base with a squid, you'd have to wear a suit resembling a plug-in Christmas tree.

One major way cats communicate is by using their eyes. This is helpful because we have eyes, too.

Cats' eyes are not exactly like ours, however. Experimenters at the University of Oregon and other bastions of great learning have wasted vats of federal funds and countless cats' lives trying to put to human use knowledge gained from interfering with cats' eye movements. It can't be done.

According to veterinary ophthalmologist Dr. Ned Buyukmihci, "Humans have a very specialized region in their retina with which they see and almost all their vision depends on that specialized area. Cats don't have that specialized area. Also, cats have a much greater ability to see at night. These and other reasons make the information from vision experiments on cats worthless and inapplicable to humans." May I suggest going to PETA.org to register your complaint that experiments like these on cats—and others—should get their funding cut off?

Veterinarian H. Ellen Whiteley reports that cats can see in light only one-fifth as bright as the faintest light we can see and that their complex ears contain 30 different muscles, whereas ours have only six. But no set of figures or charts can convey the anger, annoyance, bliss, love, and subtler emotions your cat's extraordinarily expressive eyes hold. So don't think I was scrimping on design costs when I left out the chart.

Cats' pupils dilate when they are angry or on the attack, and cats "smile" at us and other cat friends by squinting.

Your cat will slowly almost (but usually not quite) close her eyes and reopen them while looking at you. When almost closed, the eyelids are held at the lowest point for a second. You can return the sentiment by gently squinting back, mimicking the cat's pattern. It would be rude to do anything less.

If a cat closes her eyes all the way for more than a split second, that is absolute trust in action.

If your cat "smiles" when looking at you, you are observing a private contentment, expressed publicly in the same way you might give a happy sigh in an empty room.

To read eyes, you have to watch closely.

When your cat sees a bird outside the window and that tail starts twitching, compare the look in your cat's eyes to the look that accompanies a different tail-twitching experience—the appearance of a strange cat. Although your cat's eyes will dart back and forth in both cases, the first look is reserved for interest in prey, the second for interest in a potential marauder. Although the two looks are different to the seasoned cat observer, both hold elements of annoyance, keen interest, an awareness of the potential for action, reserve, and the need for vigilance.

Annoyance is commonly expressed in joint eye and tail action. If you are not attentive, you can get swatted at or bitten, simply because you missed your cat's polite warning that he or she was in no mood to be petted or picked up.

BODY LANGUAGE

Kittens who were weaned too early or who just plain miss their mothers or the pleasant sensation of nursing "make biscuits" with their feet, kneading whatever is in front of them, as if still pumping milk out of their mama's chest. If they choose to do that to you, what a high compliment indeed.

Cats in cages at animal shelters flatten their ears back in fear or as a warning, call out plaintively, and frantically push their paws through the bars. Some bat at people passing by, appealing to them in the same way any prisoner might. In less desperate surroundings— your kitchen, for instance—cats may paw at you to let you know it is past suppertime and your watch must have stopped. It is impolite to ignore being batted at, so even if the cause of the swat is not immediately apparent, try to figure it out.

Your cat also sends messages by stretching and yawning.

Of course, tense cats don't do either. Chances are, your cat feels wonderfully contented if she throws back her head, bends her spine, extends her legs, and unwinds with a yawn. Let her enjoy the feeling without being distracted.

Lions and tigers and the smallest of small cats also stretch to show off to others of their kind or to predators. Such stretches can mean, "I'm so in control here that I can relax." The show of teeth that accompanies yawning can mean "See these? Pretty big, eh? So don't try to take advantage."

Grooming is carried out for practical reasons, of course, but also to cover embarrassment. When a cat does something that doesn't quite work, like jumping up to catch a moth and missing, she may cover up her ineptitude by immediately sitting down and starting to clean herself vigorously.

It's as if your cat is saying, "That klutzy-seeming thing you just saw was actually quite purposeful. I was about to catch that moth when I remembered some grooming that needed to be done, and look, here I am doing it now." Even if Kitty does something extraordinarily silly, never laugh! Laughter is a universally understood language.

THEREIN HANGS A TAIL

A cat's tail is perhaps her most expressive body bit. If you could play jumprope with its thrashing movements, watch out! But there are few sights more pleasing than Kitty walking toward you with tail held high or making featherlike figure-eight rubs between your ankles. How joy can kink a tail like that, no one knows! Cats would make terrible poker players. Every time they got a good hand, their tail would bend like a question mark.

Slow thumping is a warning: "Look out. I'm annoyed!" Fast swishing is annoyance sitting on a springboard, ready to turn into full-fledged anger. A twitch is like a double take—neither cat nor tail knows at the moment of the twitch what will happen next.

One of PETA's rescued cats, Jack, spent his first year confined to a cat crate in a hoarder's home. Given the run of the office, he could often be found sitting and waiting for me by the elevator when I'd run out to an appointment. As soon as I stepped out, Jack would flip over onto his back, and I had to resist the urge to ruin the moment by rubbing his beautiful tiger tummy, something he hated. Instead, I would touch his head and say, "What an angel, Jack!" happy in the knowledge that he must have been content, since sad cats never roll on their backs.

What a treat it is to see cats lie on their backs and bump their rumps from side to side. I think it means they have just won the lottery. Check in the cat bed for a winning stub.

SWAPPING GIFTS

Once upon a time, a Las Vegas animal trainer named Bobby Berosini was found locking the orangutans he used in his casino performances alone in solid, stainless steel boxes between acts. The boxes were barely bigger than were the animals themselves, with no windows and only small air holes at the top.

The apes came to know that this man had the power to take them out of the box as well as to seal them away from the world and each other. Berosini permitted no one else to feed the orangutans. Small wonder that, when he let them out of their prisons, they hugged him. They saw him as not only their jailer but also their ticket to sustenance, even life itself.

Sadly, Berosini's mean treatment of the orangutans illustrates that all sentient beings will show gratitude to those who feed them, whether that person is decent and loving or exploitative and rotten.

In a loving home, cats wish to return the favor. They don't just take. They try to reciprocate. Cats who go outdoors may go to enormous trouble to bring home prey—live, dead, sometimes in bits—to present to their beloved. Bringing you the head is the cat equivalent of picking out something extra-special for you from the Neiman Marcus catalog. While I advise never to let cats out unsupervised (for inarguably solid reasons), if you do and are given an unwanted treasure as a gift, it must not go unappreciated.

Wrong response: "Jeez, will you get that thing away from me!"

Right response: "Ooooooh, thank you," followed by much appreciative petting. Then read the chapter on other reasons not to let your cat outside unsupervised and lock the door.

In nature, protocol would demand that you eat a bit of the body first, then allow the gift-giver a chance to share some. This is not recommended, unless you are prepared to have your stomach pumped and dose yourself with vermicide.

It is also incredibly rude to be seen disposing of the gift quickly or in front of the giver. Here's the protocol: If the animal is dead, try to show your appreciation by batting the body (or body bit) about. If the animal is alive, withdraw with the offering into a closed room. This will allow you to examine the body for injuries, effect release through a door or window, call a wildlife worker, or just mull things over. Kitty will assume you have sought a private place in which to admire and guard your treasure.

Dealing with these delicate situations provides yet another reason to keep Kitty safe in your home with you, rather than out there in the Wild West, shopping for a new adopted parent.

MESSY MESSAGES

Cats suffering from cystitis or a urinary tract infection—both of which can be very painful and even life-threatening—tend to urinate in odd places, sometimes particularly on a ceramic or tile surface, such as in the bath or sink. You may or may not see blood in the urine. Please, rush your cat straight to the vet for treatment. Every painful moment counts. There are, however, other reasons why you might find messes in places you do not wish to find them.

Cats—being mortal, physical, and emotional beings—can get jealous, sad, and ill. Sometimes, people don't notice. This forces the cats to resort to drastic measures to get their point across. Consider an article in New York magazine titled, "Is Your Cat Contemplating Suicide?" which asks, "Are New York's cats neurotic, dysfunctional, or just plain screwed up?" Many city cats, according to the article, are in the same sorry shape as Gus, a bear at Central Park Zoo, who went mad from boredom and stress and started to swim obsessively back and forth in his minuscule pool. The zoo put Gus on Prozac and offered professional help and toys.

In my experience, it's not just city cats or bears. Let's take a look:

Say you have recently moved, taken up going to the gym, or divorced. Perhaps there is a new baby in the house or a visiting dog. Could it be that you spend most evenings gazing, enraptured, into the eyes of a new Mr. or Ms. Right? Don't think your resident feline isn't affected. Even a new perfume can throw Kitty for a loop. If you no longer smell like you (a big deal for sensitive, scent-oriented beings), who knows what's sacred (or safe) anymore? Sadness, worry, separation anxiety, insecurity, or fits of outright, downright pique may dominate his or her mind and mood.

Some cats, particularly if there are other cats in the household, can force themselves to tolerate your new love or take your frequent absences in stride, just as your old flame may be able to play tennis with your new love without smashing Beau Number 2 with the racquet. One change that is more than any cat can take, however, is to find himself no longer allowed on the bed. Your cat believes, as did the ancient Egyptian cats, that a cat's duty is to guard you, the most cherished object of his love, from attack during your most vulnerable time.

Sometimes, a cat is reduced to making a truly desperate cry for help. This can take the form of urine or feces left on the bed or in some other spot guaranteed to capture your attention. Even a neutered male may start spraying urine. This is not an accident or a sign of stupidity or poor training. It can be a communication to you from a cat who feels that you are not listening.

Such a physical outpouring of emotional anguish should cause you to concentrate not on changing the cat's behavior but rather on modifying your own. Your cat could be telling you that he is physically ill and needs emergency assistance (see above) or feels left out, betrayed, scorned, miserable over the loss of someone, or abandoned. If it is the latter, you must be convincing in showing that you still feel the same love and affection for him you always did and that he still holds a most special place in your heart. Punishment has no place here.

If that means arranging that special dinner for two at your home, rather than going to a restaurant, or inviting the team over to watch sports videos, instead of always hitting the courts, don't waiver. You made a commitment to your cat first, and that must mean something.

Introduce your new love, whether baby or boyfriend, to your cat now, no matter how long all this has been going on. Kitty needs to see that you are proud of him, so stroke and praise your cat in front of the new love.

Most cats can, if begrudgingly, accept that you are so weak-willed and emotionally needy that you may seek another source of affection. What is totally unforgivable is for you to lavish attention on someone else *to the exclusion* of your cat.

Never, ever allow yourself or a friend to push your cat off the couch or bed or to say words equivalent to "Go away," even during the most amorous moments. Respectfully work around your cat until your cat decides to go away of his own accord, no matter how long it takes. You don't want your cat to go around with a chip the size of Mount Rushmore on his shoulder.

CAT GOT YOUR TONGUE?

Hank Ketchum said, "Meow is like Aloha. It can mean anything." Most of us who recognize the basics of cat lingo would disagree with Mr. Ketchum. There is the long, mournful call of the lonely young female; the spitting sounds of the fighting male; the chirpy half purr, half mew that greets you when you come home; and the scream of pain when a paw accidentally gets underfoot. It's the rich language of more subtle conveyance in between that escapes us.

Answering back, even if you get it wrong, is usually appreciated. Any return sound means, "I hear you. I am responding." Best of all, if Kitty understands your language as little as you understand "cat," she may think the miscommunication is all on her side and blame herself.

Cat photographer Elizabeth Cyran believes cats use methods of communication of a higher order than we are able to understand. Says Elizabeth, "Look at the pictures abductees draw of the aliens who they say captured them. They are cats! They signal the mother ship late at night. They know things we don't. They communicate without words. I vowed I would never share my life with a cat. They were nasty, clawed the furniture and smelled. Now I know how wrong I have been. Life without a cat is no life!"

Well, whether or not cats are communicating in other ways, cat sounds can be heard with the ear and the heart. Enjoy the music of the sound, and sing back. I have had long conversations with some of the cats who have shared my home and have yet to be committed. If they hear you respond, they will invariably try something back, and on it goes. You are like musicians "spelling" each other in alternate riffs, cooperating, in touch, even if each keeps his own tune.

Talking back is especially helpful to your cat if she is calling out in distress, panic, or worry, perhaps stuck on a high ledge or in the car on the way to the vet. Your answer says, "I am here. It's going to be all right." Your words will have the same reassuring effect the rescue worker's voice has on a person trapped in a collapsed building. Whether or not everything will turn out all right may be anyone's guess, but for the moment you can provide comfort and calm your cat down.

Contrary to the opinion of Barbara Holland, someone quoted as saying, "By and large, people who enjoy teaching animals to roll over will find themselves happier with a dog," respectful interaction with a cat can be as beneficial to the cat as to the human initiating the lesson.

Use the same sentences consistently and often. If you have a special way of announcing food or a supervised walk, your cat will become used to not so much the words as the length, sound, and tone of the sentence. Listen to yourself when you talk about routine events, then try the same words in the same tone and feeling—but in a different place and without other signals. If you can evoke the right response (e.g., your cat jumps up to speed into the kitchen, although you've said, "Let's see what's for dinner," in the den and without touching the can opener), you're on the right track. Develop one, then two, then more key communicative sentences and see how it goes.

Finding Your Inner Purr was the name of an old audiocassette, subtitled "The Cat Lover's Guide to Relaxation." Newspaper reviewer Wendy Christensen relates that when she played the tape for the second time, Dandelion, one of her cats, "seemed to pay unusually close attention, snuggling up next to me near the stereo speaker, something she rarely does." This 20-pound wild cat look-alike with a temperament to match seemed progressively mellower as the tape played, especially side two, which advocated purring along with your cat. Christensen felt silly doing it but bravely followed the directions, breathing and purring along with the narrator. She reports that Dandelion, who was usually unreceptive (the nice term) to having her triple-thick, easily matted fur groomed, was so relaxed that she purred as Christensen worked a comb through it.

PROFESSIONAL HELP

Anyone can teach a cat not to jump on the counter (put citrus deodorant spray, double-sided tape, or plain old water on it until Kitty hangs it up) or a kitten how to use his litter box (place him in there gently and work his front paws in a scratching motion). But if your cat develops behavior that you cannot figure out and do not wish to live with, perhaps it's time to consult a cat behaviorist. Be sure you pick one who is certified, not certifiable. As with dog walkers, there are some dangerous, know-nothing shingle-hangers out there.

Of course, certification *guarantees* nothing, but it does mean the consultant either has passed an associate course in applied animal behavior or, better, is an applied animal behaviorist. It also means the consultant is supposed to abide by ethical standards imposed by the Animal Behavior Society.

Only a few dozen such behaviorists have expertise in cat stuff (not the technical term). Ask for references, as with any veterinarian, and check online and with your local Better Business Bureau and animal protection organizations to see if anyone has lodged complaints about the consultant.

Most important, walk out if they seem impatient with the patient or suggest anything you wouldn't do to yourself.

12
BEWARE: CATS CAN SUFFER SILENTLY

If ever domesticated cats manage to get a Bill of Basic Rights through Congress—and I wouldn't put it past them to do so one day—the right to decent healthcare could top the list of their entitlements. It would appear directly above a cat's inalienable right not to be moved from your lap, even though he has somehow been magically transformed into a 50-pound lump that has cut off all circulation in your legs.

Who can concentrate on love or pretty much anything else when they feel awful? You know what I mean if you've ever tried to have a conversation with someone suffering from a migraine. They are utterly incapable of concentrating on anything other than their burning desire to have you stop talking and go somewhere else. Your cat's the same way.

Perhaps one of the worst things that can happen to a cat besides falling asleep in the clothes dryer (yes, this happens—see chapter 15) is for no one to notice that he has developed a physical problem.

It's hard to imagine cats as the strong, silent type, given that they can yowl up a storm if someone steps on a body part. However, like most wild or fairly newly domesticated beings, who are aware that predators put you on their dance card if you announce your vulnerability, they tend to clam up rather than cry out when they are in a really bad way.

What happens if you wake up with a toothache, develop a 10-ton headache, or suffer from arthritis? Unless you are a Navy S.E.A.L. on active maneuvers, it is a safe bet that you will promptly seek relief. But what if you couldn't? Put yourself in your cat's place. Imagine being in pain and discovering that no one notices and that you can't communicate your condition to them.

Because pain is invisible, a mental event, this can be the frightening reality cats face when things go quietly physically wrong for them.

Consider Roger, a handsome, neutered male cat who lived with my friend Kim. Roger developed a nasty disposition. He no longer enjoyed being petted, and sometimes he hissed at Kim or even scratched him when Kim rubbed his head affectionately. He had become intolerant of the family dog and of visitors. Kim attributed this impatience to advanced age and simply complained back to his cat.

One day, Kim had to take Roger to the vet for a routine immunization. He happened to moan to the vet that his cat had become a grumpy old man. The vet asked a few questions and then put Roger on the clinic floor to test his ability to find his way about. The old cat didn't do very well.

Now, Kim was no ordinary cat owner. He was a veteran animal rights campaigner who had spent all his adult life trying to help animals. You can imagine how chagrined he felt when the vet announced that Roger had been seriously ill for some time. He suspected that there was a tumor growing on Roger's brain.

In fact, there was, and the tumor was causing problems with Roger's vision, but because the cat knew every twist and turn in his home, Kim hadn't noticed anything wrong. The pressure from the tumor also caused Roger considerable pain, especially when anyone touched his head or neck. That is why he hissed, moved away, and, when people were persistent, even bit or scratched. His pathetic acts of self-defense had been mistaken for nastiness and had been met with disappointment and reprimands.

Something more common—but even more dangerous— happened to Humphrey, a cat who lived with Diana, a lawyer friend of mine.

Diana had been working hard on an important case, staying at the office until very late at night, then dashing back to work again as soon as she could get out of bed in the mornings.

She had simply not been around enough to notice that Humphrey had started to use the litter box frequently. She wasn't there to see that he sometimes returned to the box within a few minutes of his last visit or to hear his tiny, reserved "mew" when he strained to urinate. She hadn't had time to play with him or notice the new, pained expression on his face.

Every morning, Diana carefully dumped the contents of Humphrey's litter pan into a bag and refilled the tray. She noticed nothing because the litter absorbed the evidence of Humphrey's distress.

Then one morning, Diana jumped into the shower and found tiny drops of bloody urine on the porcelain. Humphrey had found a way to let her know he was in trouble. Still, Diana didn't realize how deep that trouble was. Calling from her office, she made an appointment to take Humphrey to the vet the next day, not suspecting for a moment that Humphrey was in agony, his urethra blocked.

The next morning, when Diana walked into the bathroom, she found Humphrey lying motionless on the floor. He had gone into shock. His painful bladder infection, which can afflict male and female cats alike, had caused systemic poisoning. Despite immediate surgery, Humphrey did not pull through.

Within the week, a far more vigilant Diana noticed that her other cat, Rayette, was straining to pass urine. This time, Diana was on the way to the vet within minutes. Her cat had cystitis, which sometimes goes through a household of felines, and Diana's immediate response spared Rayette any of Humphrey's pain as well as her life.

Sometimes serious illness can escape even the most conscientious souls, like Kim. When you hear yourself say, "Isn't he well-behaved today?" or "Doesn't that cat sleep a lot!" or "Boy, he doesn't usually do that!" you could be noticing that your cat is run-down, weak, not feeling very well, unable to move about comfortably, or otherwise in distress.

Any change in a cat's pattern of behavior or mood merits some thought and a closer look right away.

I recommend doing the following every day (not because you really need to do it that often but because your cat will love it):

1 **Run your hand smoothly from stem to stern along Kitty's body,** feeling gently for lumps and bumps, seeing if your cat appears sensitive to the touch anywhere, and parting the hair to check for fleas, hair loss, an ear infection, you name it. This is the kitty equivalent of getting a back rub every day and will bond your cat to you like glue.

2 **Look into your cat's eyes.** Don't forget to blink adoringly or your cat will think you have gone off the deep end. Are the eyes weepy? Is the skin inside the eye at the inner corner covering part of the eye, rather than being almost imperceptible and flat? That is your cat's nictitating membrane, and it may be trying to tell you that Kitty is under the weather and that further investigation is in order.

3 **Very gently pull back the skin around Kitty's gums** (while rubbing his face for fun) and see how those teeth are doing. Do they need cleaning? (If so, see chapter on mouth health.) If the gums are white or very pale, your cat could have parasites or be anemic for some other reason.

4 **Sniff Kitty's breath.** Is that home cooking, or is something rotten?

5 Sneak a peek under Kitty's tail. This is a delicate maneuver that can cause deep, lasting offense, so take it easy. It may work to incorporate the under-tail inspection into some serious rump scratching, which will make your cat raise his tail. Is everything clean and shipshape? Or are there surprises, e.g., a prolapsed rectum (the skin has popped out and is distended) or the sort of untidiness that can mean parasites or an upset tummy?

6 Squeeze each toe very, very gently, until the nails come out and you can look for breakages or abnormalities.

7 Look (and smell) inside ears. If you see gunk, put a tiny bit of mineral oil on a cotton swab and wipe gently. If those black dots move or jump, you'll need ear mite medicine. These mites particularly annoy the owner of the ear. We know this because a human researcher actually placed cat ear mites in his own ears just to see how things went. He woke up with a start at 3 a.m. every morning as the mites got an early and vigorous start to their day! To deal with them, you will have to dig all around inside your cat's cavernous, convoluted ears extremely gently, and that is a big job. Infection greets your nose with a little zing and requires analysis before a remedy can be chosen. If your cat digs in an ear or two or shakes his head a lot, take that as a sign that there is a problem that deserves attention.

8 Rub your fingers lightly under and between your cat's paw pads in case a Spanish doubloon or burr is uncomfortably lodged there and could lead to infection.

9 Look at Kitty's hair coat. See if it is shiny (not greasy, which is a sign of ill health) and has elasticity, i.e., if you take up a fold of skin on Kitty's back and then let go, it knows where it is supposed to be and springs right back where it belongs. If the skin "sits there" or very slowly returns to take its place as part of the greater cat body, your cat may be dehydrated. Is that automatic water dispenser clogged (throw it out anyway in favor of a stainless steel bowl you can clean and fill daily with fresh water), or could your cat be suffering from

diarrhea? If the coat is dull, perhaps a stool sample should be dropped off at the vet's. If the coat is dry, perhaps your angel's diet would benefit from more fresh, steamed vegetables (see chapter 16) and a drop of vegetable oil, like olive oil. Bathing a cat's outside bits will not restore a cat's inside bits, so look for the cause before choosing the cure. A handy tool is the Plastic Pet Hair Shedding Grooming Brush, which is available at PETA.org/GroomingBrush.

10 **Brush away excess hair** with any effective brush from a pet supply store or catalog. Most cats prefer plastic to metal—there's something scary about steel. Perhaps it reminds them of ships. If you don't brush, cats can ingest wads of hair when they lick their coats clean. Hairballs may make good material for standup comics, but they aren't digestible and can clog up a cat's innards, causing nasty, knotty problems. Here's one sign of them: Your cat stretches his neck out, crouches low to the ground, and coughs, usually with little to no result. Your vet can give you a malty-tasting lubricant that will help or possibly Miralax, but routine brushing and a good diet works just as well for most cats.

Can You Prevent Kidney Disease Through Diet?

TOP **TIP**

Here's a scary fact: The majority of cats will come down with kidney disease* at some point in their lifetime. And kidney disease is awful for them, so please do all you can to guard against it.

***Read labels carefully.** The commonly accepted theory used to be that a high ash content in commercial food caused kidney disease, and wet food was recommended because it's lower in ash. If you're feeding commercial food, it's still wise to stay away from dry food, if only because your cat needs to take in liquids to help her kidneys function properly. Today's thinking is that high phosphorus and protein contents are likely culprits, so reading labels is important. The Association of American Feed Control Officials guidelines for phosphorus in foods for healthy cats are 1.25 grams per 1,000 calories for maintenance and 2 grams per 1,000 calories for growth. Remember that these levels are for normal diets. If your cat already has chronic kidney disease, you want to keep the levels significantly lower.

Here are some good guidelines to follow:
• Switch to wet food and avoid dry, as it makes the kidneys work harder.
• Introduce Kitty to low-phosphorus, fresh foods like watermelon, apples, bananas, green beans, carrots, broccoli, zucchini, and blueberries.

- Add milk thistle to support kidney health (you can buy it in cat-friendly flavors). It contains silymarin, which helps the kidneys filter out toxins more efficiently.
- Make sure the water dish is always full and meticulously clean and the water is fresh to encourage her to drink and, in so doing, flush her kidneys. Consider purchasing a fountain, which many cats love to drink from.
- Symptoms of kidney disease include drinking more than usual, increased urination, more frequent trips to the litter box, going off her food, vomiting, losing interest in grooming, and a dry hair coat that lacks elasticity. Get to a vet right away for a solid diagnosis.

Tip on the geriatric cat: Elderly cats can suffer from joint pain and feel the damp in the same way that old timers' joints can predict if it's going to rain. They may not be as agile in their dotage, either, so we must not just keep them warm and shield them from drafts, which can whip along at floor level, but also be sure they have cozy bedding that they can reach without mountaineering gear. A cat bed with sides three-quarters of the way around, either store-bought or fashioned from a cardboard box filled with soft material, does the trick, especially if it's raised off the floor but not too high. Also, consider purchasing ramps or footstools to help old-timers reach the heights that were previously attainable in their youth—such as that cozy spot on the couch or the bed.

A cardinal rule: When it comes to your beloved's health, there are two good slogans to adopt—"Better safe than sorry" and "Better a vet than a regret." If in doubt as to your cat's condition, contact your vet. If a telephone chat with the vet or the vet's assistant doesn't satisfy you or solve the problem, go to the clinic. If the condition is anything more serious than a hangnail or a hairball, do not put off the visit for even a day. And if your vet isn't helpful, don't hesitate to get a different one. Go to the emergency clinic if your regular vet is closed.

13
IF KITTY MUST GO TO A NEW HOME

One hopes you will never have cause to use this chapter, but cats happen, and sadly, it is not always possible to offer a permanent home to every one of them who crosses your path. Cats descend on some people with the regularity of birthdays, which seem to come more and more often these days. My mother believes that some of us have a "VACANCY" sign on our doors that can be seen only by people and animals who are down on their luck. Unlike motel signs, we can't change it to "FULL."

Many years ago on a bitterly cold winter day, not the sort of weather you'd want to change a tire in, I was driving along a country road, my mind completely uncluttered with thoughts of cats. I wasn't on my way to meet the Pope, but I did have an appointment that was scheduled to begin at a particular time, as appointments usually do. Of course, such commitments mean nothing to a cat.

The road I was on had been plowed after a severe snowstorm, but beyond the asphalt, every field and bush was covered with ice. The temperature was in the teens, and the wind blew wafer-thin sheets of snow and ice onto the car as I drove along.

I was flicking the wipers on and off, trying to push off the icy muck spattering up on my windshield, when I noticed that, at the very edge of the road, the all-encompassing whiteness had been interrupted for a split second by a tiny flash of orange and black.

"I thawt I thaw a ... guinea pig?"

Braking cautiously on this skating rink of a road, I stopped the car and backed up until I saw that flash of colors again. There was a ball of fluff, certainly the size of a guinea pig and with the same long, coarse hair in the same colors as a guinea pig—but not a guinea pig at all.

When I stopped, the ball unwound itself to become a tiny kitten. I opened the car door and leaned over to scoop her up. She didn't run. I don't think she could have. Her little body was doing the jitterbug so hard from the cold that I could actually hear her teeth rattle. Her whiskers were covered with ice, and little icicle tears ran from her eyes down to her chin. Her long calico coat was blowing like a polar bear's coat in the bitter wind.

"Mew," she said, in the angry, anxious, pitiful voice of a desperate, betrayed little being. She glared and pleaded at the same time as if to say, "Please save me. This is a very cruel joke, and I do not wish to be part of it anymore. Do you understand?"

As small as she was, I felt pretty small myself. After all, it was one of my species who had chucked this vulnerable little kitten out into the freezing tundra in the middle of nowhere and then gone back to somewhere warm.

That was in the days of yore, before mobile phones, so back we went to my house to cancel the appointment and crank up the heat. Soon, "Campus" was fast asleep, curled up between the pillows on my bed, toasty-warm and well fed, having wolfed down the equivalent of her own bodyweight in vittles. The other cats were barred from entry and sat in a big cat heap outside the door, pouting like a band of Brigitte Bardots.

Campus did get to stay, but I knew that the next cat through the door could not. There really was no room left at my inn, unless I sacrificed the mental health and physical well-being of the rest of the troupe. Crowding leads to stress. The "I'm tired of being a small fish in a big pond" syndrome affects a cat's immune system, and respiratory viruses, cystitis, and other health problems have less trouble getting their foot in Kitty's door. Other options had to be explored.

Finding the right home for a needy cat is harder than persuading Donald Trump to become a Democrat. With Trump, you'd have to be really tough, but with cat placement you have to be tougher. You have to soak your resolve in 3-in-One Oil. That's because the words "I'll take that cat" do not guarantee a good home, and "I promise to give him a good home" can be a promise not worth the paper it isn't written on.

I can't adopt a positive, Julie Andrews–like frame of mind on all this, because my experience as a humane officer has made me realistic. If compassionate people could see what eventually becomes of so many of their well-intentioned placements, they would realize that finding a truly good and lasting home is a bit like searching for the Holy Grail. My advice is to make a promise to yourself that you will never risk your cat's happiness by settling for anything less than a home you are *sure* is excellent.

If the prospective adopter cannot satisfy all the requirements outlined in "Guidelines on Finding a New Home for Your Cat" in this chapter, taking Kitty to a *good* shelter (see below) is a safer option. It may be a horrible fact, but it's a fact nonetheless.

Again, taking Kitty to a decently run shelter where she'll have a chance of a good placement or at least a kind end is far better for the cat than foisting that unwanted feline onto a casual taker.

An old Chinese proverb contends that if you save a person's life, you are responsible for it. Well, if you save nine lives, the same responsibility applies. A bad home—where Kitty's pain may go unnoticed, where she is left vulnerable to passing cars and delinquents, and where she becomes a breeding machine, churning out offspring into a world in which so many go homeless—is not better than going to heaven or that great void in the sky. I'm not happy to say this, but if you face the options honestly, it's true.

Do cats have souls? Well, there is no final authority here to ask, so opinions differ. If you think they do, then passing peacefully from this world cannot be such a horrid fate, especially for the innocent victim of unprovoked meanness. If you think cats do not have souls, then all the more reason to make sure every moment they spend in this, their only life, is pleasant. If we ourselves cannot give them happiness, they deserve a wonderful placement or, at least, a ticket off the planet.

FINDING THE RIGHT HOME FOR YOUR CAT

You care about this cat, of course, and so you must find him a truly good home. But remember that not every inquirer will share your understanding and concerns. The following will provide the information you need to select a good home and help ensure that the cat you place will still be cared for properly next year and even 18 or 20 years from now.

BEFORE YOU MAKE THAT BIG DECISION

Are you reluctant to part with an old friend (or, for that matter, a new friend) but feeling that you have no choice? Be sure to explore all your options before taking the big step. Once an animal leaves your care, can you be absolutely certain he will be safe and treated well for the rest of his life?

If your cat is having behavior problems, consult a veterinarian first to make sure illness isn't the root cause, as it may be. If your cat is given a clean bill of health, try a certified behaviorist or humane trainer. Don't hesitate to call local humane groups or PETA for advice.

Having financial difficulties or traveling for an extended period of time? Ask a family member or trusted friend to care for your cat temporarily. Also, humane rescue groups may agree to foster your friend, but again, go and look at the facility to see where and how he will be kept.

Having trouble finding an apartment that allows animals? Try networking through local humane societies and animal rights groups. Post ads in veterinarians' offices, companion animal supply stores, and health food stores. Go online. Beg your prospective landlord to make an exception: Evoke testimony as to your goodness from previous landlords, add an extra deposit, or even offer to wash your landlord's car on weekends. Show off a photo of your cat looking enormously humble, cute, very small, and totally harmless—much the way you might behave in front of the judge at traffic court. If you are threatened with eviction over an animal companion, the Animal Legal Defense Fund may be able to help. And PETA may be able to help you, too, as sometimes you have legal rights you didn't even imagine.

Allergies? Try these tips:

- Have someone who is not allergic brush the cat every few days.
- Run a warm, damp cloth over your cat's coat every few days to pick up extra dander.
- Change your furnace and air filters often, choosing the finest possible mesh recommended by the manufacturer to keep dander from floating about in circulated air.
- Wash anything you can as often as you can. Avoid shag or high-pile carpeting.
- Get a high-quality air purifier that removes cat dander and other bits and bobs from your atmosphere. There are lots of models available.

GUIDELINES ON FINDING A NEW HOME FOR YOUR CAT

Here are some basic questions designed to give you necessary information about a potential adopter's attitude and level of responsibility.

1 *Why do you want a cat?*
Look for someone who wants an animal to be part of the family as a household companion. Beware of anyone who may want a cat, especially a "purebred" one, for breeding. They want money, not a cat. If someone wants the cat as a gift for a friend or relative, insist that the person who will spend the next decade or more with the cat be involved in the selection. No cat or any other animal should be a surprise gift. The surprise may be that the recipient doesn't want the cat and the cat finds himself resented or homeless again. If a child calls, ask to speak with his parents.

2 *Have you had cats before? What happened to them?*
People who have never had cats before should be advised of the considerable expense and responsibility involved in caring for them, including exercise, feed bills, and veterinary costs, which ain't cheap. Someone who has had several animals stolen, killed by cars, lost, or given away is undoubtedly a poor prospect and should be summarily dismissed from consideration.

3 *If you move or travel, what will happen to the cat?*
Caring for a cat can be a 20-year (or more) commitment. Remind prospects that they will have to make arrangements for someone to care for the cat during vacations and must plan for the animal's needs if contemplating a move. Ask what arrangements will be made in those circumstances.

4 *Will you allow the cat outdoors?*
This is a trick question. If the answer is an unqualified yes, don't trust the person to keep the cat safe from the streets unless you genuinely believe in the power of instant reeducation of adults.

5 *How do you feel about spaying/neutering?*
More than 20 million companion animals are destroyed each year because there are simply not enough good homes to go around. Always require that the prospective owner pay to spay or neuter before adoption to avoid further breeding, resulting in more

homeless animals. (Veterinarians can spay and neuter kittens when they are just 6 to 8 weeks old.) If you or the prospect are concerned about sterilization costs, call your local humane organization to find out about reduced-fee programs. Be cautious if people already have an unaltered animal in their home, as they may have breeding in mind. Try to sterilize the cat before placement.

6 *Do you own or rent your home?*
If the prospect does not own, see if her lease permits cats. Thousands of animals are given up each year after being discovered by the owner of the property. Just because everyone is violating the rules doesn't mean that the boom won't be lowered on the animals whose people are getting away with it now.

7 *Who else lives in your home?*
Make certain that all other members of the household want a cat and are aware of the caller's plans by talking to them yourself. Also, determine the ages of any children in the household. Families with young children should be told that normal kitten and cat play often includes jumping, kicking, and biting and that cats must be protected from rambunctious children.

WHAT TO DO IF YOU ARE UNABLE TO FIND A GOOD HOME

Please don't rush into a placement because you are pressured by time, and don't skimp on the questions you ask prospective adopters, even if they seem to think them excessive. They are not. If you are unable to find an *excellent* home for your cat, be brave and take her to an animal shelter operated by a reputable humane organization. Choose a shelter that (a) checks out prospective homes carefully by doing home checks, (b) requires spaying or neutering, (c) does not give away or *sell* animals to research institutions, (d) does not shunt cats into hoarders' homes just to make their euthanasia rates look low, and (e) uses a painless sodium pentobarbital injection intravenously if euthanasia becomes necessary, just as good veterinarians do.

Face it: A painless death is far better than a cruel, slow death by disease, exposure, starvation, or being crushed under the wheels of a car—and better than a life made hellish by negligence or cruelty. A peaceful end is certainly preferable to being turned out onto the street or locked up in a bathroom, garage, or basement where fresh air, proper food, clean water, exercise, regular health care, companionship, respect, and love are in short supply.

If your animal friend is old, extremely shy, or dependent on you and you cannot find a home with someone he trusts and loves, the kindest course may lie in taking him to a veterinarian or shelter to be euthanized. An animal who has been with you for a long time is likely to suffer and pine terribly when you are gone. When I went to Ireland for four months and left my beloved Jarvis with my best friend, after I returned, he wouldn't speak to me for about as many months as I had been gone. He obviously thought I'd deserted him, that I simply didn't care. Cats may have short attention spans, but they have long memories. Their hearts break just as ours do.

As a final kindness, remain in the room to comfort your old friend during euthanasia.

Never sell or give a cat or kitten to a pet shop. People operating pet shops are obviously in it for the money and have no concern whatsoever about the fate of the animals after they leave the store. Without a thorough screening process, kittens are sold to people buying on impulse and to people who are unfit to care for an animal, even to psychopaths looking for a kitten to abuse. When Kim Novak cradled a Siamese cat in her arms in the movie *Bell, Book and Candle*, Siamese cat sales soared, only to be followed by a huge influx of Siamese cats at pounds and shelters.

WARNING!
There are people who acquire cats to sell to laboratories. These

folks are often quite cunning and pretend to seek animals as family companions. They may bring children or senior citizens with them to gain your confidence. In Los Angeles, Bob and Elsie Anderson lived at the desert's edge. Soon after moving there, they discovered people using the desert as a favorite dumping ground for unwanted animals.

Bob and Elsie found the courage to go into the desert and retrieve these animals in various stages of deterioration, pull the cactus needles from their paws and noses, and make expensive and inconvenient trips to the vet. With unfailing mercy, they returned these animals' lives to them.

Eleven cats and nine dogs later, the Andersons realized their home had reached its carrying capacity. They didn't stop rescuing animals, but rather than taking them off to the shelter, they chose instead to find them homes by placing giveaway ads.

Enter now Mrs. Pierce (her real name). She seemed like a nice little old lady, and she explained to Elsie that her husband had died recently and that she very much wanted a dog to keep her company. Before relinquishing the dog to Mrs. Pierce, Elsie requested visitation rights. Of course she could visit the dog, Mrs. Pierce replied.

A week passed before Elsie called to ask how things were going. The dog is fine, she was told. After a few more days, Elsie made her first visit. Mrs. Pierce wasn't home, but one of her neighbors was, and when Elsie stopped to chat with him, she traveled that difficult path from the sheltered world of innocence to the grim reality of experience. From that conversation, she learned that Mrs. Pierce's son, a dealer registered with the U.S. Department of Agriculture (USDA), earned his living selling cats and dogs to laboratories.

Bob and Elsie took their case to every authority they could think of, hoping to find someone who would help them get their dog back. No one took an interest. In sheer desperation, Elsie and Bob went down the list of giveaway ads in the paper and called every person who had listed one. They found 14 people who had delivered animals into Mrs. Pierce's hands, including one woman who released two cats—a mother and her daughter, both recently spayed—on the condition that they would not be separated.

With renewed determination, the Andersons resumed their search for help. Finally, they found a USDA official who agreed to look for the animals. Of the 14, he found four. One was dead. The other three, Tippy, Spike, and Duke, were found in holding areas still waiting for laboratory assignment. The vocal cords of all three had been severed. Teeth on both sides of young Tippy's mouth had been knocked out, undoubtedly as a result of rough handling during the debarking procedure. Their experience left the three of them psychologically scarred; the slow progress back to health would demand the patience of Job and consistent, hard work on the part of those caring for them. Furthermore, their physical condition was in tatters. You could count every bone in their bodies, and their nostrils were caked with mucus.

The moral of the story is this: **Don't think this can't happen to you or the cat whose future you hold in your hands.**

Always ask for identification. (Legitimate callers will not object when you tell them why.) Write down the person's full name and driver's license number, and explain that you will visit her home (to ensure that she actually lives there—and yes, you actually will do this before adoption). Ask for (and check) references from veterinarians, landlords, neighbors, and employers. Most important, if you are advertising your animal, never say, "Free to a good home," the favorite five words of "bunchers" (those intermediaries who sell animals to laboratories).

Finally, always charge a fee. If the adopter cannot afford to cover the cost of neutering, for example, where will this precious cat end up if he requires serious (expensive) medical care later?

Adoption Checklist

• Visit the prospective adopter's home before adoption. Ask

to meet the other members of the family, and observe their reactions to the animal. Be wary of the parent who says, "Johnny will be responsible for the cat," since this could mean that no one will provide regular care or the animal will be given away when Johnny loses interest. Never feel pressured to leave the animal!

- Make sure the adopter understands the basics of responsible animal care, including ID tags, microchipping, veterinary care, leashes, and secure surroundings. Stipulations, such as spaying or neutering, need to be put in writing and signed by the adopter, but always try to sterilize the cat before placement.

- *Don't hand over your cat until you are completely satisfied.* If you have any doubts about the adopter or the potential new home or if the situation feels wrong in any other way, don't be afraid to say, "No" or "Let me think about it." Your cat friend's happiness and life depend on your fortitude.

- To ease the transition, send along toys, leashes, collars, harnesses, scratching posts, and carriers. Books and leaflets on cat care are also helpful.

- Leave your name, address, and home and work numbers and all other contact information with the adopter, insisting that they get in touch if they have any questions or problems. After the adoption, make at least one unannounced trip to the new home to make sure the cat is happy and well cared for.

Security

Make sure the cat is wearing a collar and an ID tag with your number and the number of the new owner, and, if possible, microchip Kitty in advance. Write the owner's name, phone number, and address on the outside of the collar in indelible ink. Advise the new owner not to leave the cat unattended at first, as a sense of belonging takes time to develop. A cat who has never before urinated outside the litter box, hid under furniture, or hissed at the family may do so in strange surroundings or when stressed or pining.

Be Kind to Your Local Animal Shelter

As a caring person, you will probably be upset to hear that in just one week at any large animal shelter, roughly the same number of people you could find at a ballgame dispose of their cats as casually as they might toss out a paper cup. The difference is that they accompany the deed with these eight little words: "You won't put him to sleep, will you?" This utterance allows them to step out of the door again into the sunlight and get on with their busy lives, having nicely shifted the burden of guilt from themselves to the poor soul at the animal intake desk. Shelter staff are often the innocent whipping boys for society's major shortcomings in the "how to care for animals" category. So please be kind to the people with this difficult and thankless job.

How to Find a Decent Animal Shelter

Leave nothing to faith. Call first, then if you get the right answers, go visit sans the cat. You do not want to leave a nice kitty in a nasty place.

Here's what to ask:

1 *What do you require of a new adopter?* Do not accept less than the following:

a) Sterilization, preferably *before* the cat is released (Of course, if you can accomplish this before passing Kitty on, that would be very helpful, but make sure Kitty has enough recovery time before entering a shelter, where he may be exposed to viruses from other cats.)

b) A pre-adoption home check

c) Adoption fee and reimbursement for shots and sterilization, if not already performed (If the adopter cannot afford these start-up expenses, will Kitty find himself thumbing a ride to the vet when he suddenly needs an expensive operation—as if there were any other kind?)

d) A signed contract allowing the shelter to reclaim the cat if the home is not suitable and prohibiting declawing and letting the cat go outside without supervision

e) For renters, a lease that allows cats (If it does not, Kitty may have to walk the plank the next time the adopter's landlord comes a-knockin'.)

2 *Would you ever release animals to laboratories or dealers?*
This should be a clear, unequivocal "Never." No waffling allowed. Some pounds and shelters still hand over cats to medical colleges for hands-on courses or—even in this day and age of organs-on-a-chip and whole human DNA on the internet—long-term experiments involving fear, nausea, pain, and the workings of the eyes or brain (this means electrodes are implanted in the cat's skull). As one famous poster says, "It's Not the Cat Who Needs Her Head Examined!"

3 *What method of euthanasia do you use?*
The correct answer is "an intravenous (into the vein) injection of sodium pentobarbital." This method is absolutely painless, and animals lose consciousness in two to three seconds. Other chemicals can cause discomfort or are downright painful and are, therefore, not acceptable. If the person you are dealing with rattles off the brand name of a drug, ask, "Is that sodium pentobarbital or something else?" If it's "something else," express your disappointment and proceed to another facility. If they say it is sodium pentobarbital but don't mention how they administer it, ask. Intravenously is the only acceptable way.

4 *Do you allow someone bringing in an animal for euthanasia to stay in the room with the animal?*
Even though you are probably not planning to avail yourself of this service, the answer to such a question can help you judge the facility. The best shelters actually encourage people to be with their animals

when they receive that last injection. To be that open shows that staff know that what goes on in the back room is viewable, which is good for the animal and his human. Having a loved one, not just strangers, in the room can calm an animal in distress, and the grieving human will always be able to be comforted in the knowledge that everything went well during their beloved companion's last moments.

A Word About 'No-Kill' Facilities

"No-kill" shelters may sound like an attractive option, but because they do not euthanize animals except under extreme circumstances, beware! Some of them are extremely good, but many others are houses of horror—Bates Motels for animals. Visit without your cat and look as well as listen, then ask yourself, "Is this really a safe, welcoming, kind, and promising place for me to leave my cat?" Because they must limit the number of animals they accept, most "no-kill" shelters take in only highly attractive, young, or "purebred" animals, turning away the neediest, such as the sick, the old, and the pregnant. Those end up at open-admission facilities, which are then forced to euthanize, rather than slamming the door shut.

At some "no-kill" shelters, unadoptable animals end up living in cages for years. They invariably become withdrawn, severely depressed, and "unhousetrained" and can acquire antisocial behavior that further decreases their chances of being adopted. They are the living dead—sentenced to life imprisonment with no chance of parole and no happy moments in the sun. If one cat in a cage of 50 gets cystitis, will anyone notice before it's too late? Well-meaning people who take on the huge physical and financial responsibilities of a "no-kill" shelter can find themselves overwhelmed very quickly, and too often the animals suffer from lack of individual care and attention. Too many "no-kill" shelters to count have been shut down by humane law enforcement after casual neglect turned into blatant cruelty. Others simply hand animals over to any takers—without checking to ensure that they do not end up in a laboratory or a hoarder's cage in the basement.

14

NO, YOUR CAT CAN'T GO OUT ALONE

"You must never go down to the end of the town, if you don't go down with me." If A.A. Milne had meant cats when he wrote those lines, he would definitely have been dispensing good advice. Never let your cat out without you, unless you have escape-proofed your yard. If that sounds over the top to you, Dr. David Epstein, a veterinarian in Glenview, Illinois, warns that "at least 85 percent" of the thousands of cats he treated in his practice over a 40-year span were brought in by owners who let their cats roam free.

Here is a partial list of what a cat misses by staying indoors, courtesy of the San Francisco SPCA:

- Fights with other cats
- Fights with dogs
- Fights with raccoons and skunks
- Infections from puncture wounds
- Thrown bottles or rocks
- Fleas, ticks, and worms
- Being stolen
- Being hit by a car
- Feline leukemia and feline immunodeficiency viruses
- Steel-jaw leghold traps
- Rat bait poisoning
- Pesticide poisoning

I can vouch for the fact that this list is partial. What I have seen cats endure has cured me of letting cats onto the street, ever.

Here is just a small taste: As a humane officer, I had the job of collecting the remains of a cat who had been ritually tortured and mutilated by juveniles who thought it was cool to play at being in a satanic cult. Another time, I picked up a cat whose head was full of metal staples put there with considerable ingenuity by a bored and sadistic transient. That cat lived, but another cat who wandered by a garden floor apartment during a party didn't. It was no consolation to the cat that the court sentenced to jail the young man who did the deed. He had swung that poor cat repeatedly against the wall and then buried him, still breathing, in the woods behind the complex. I could go on, but as I say, the list is endless and depressing. It is one reason PETA maintains a 24/7 cruelty hotline at 757-756-4450.

Of course, birds, insects, mice, and moles will miss your newly indoor cat but in the best of ways. The toll cats exact on free-living animals is phenomenal. It is conservatively estimated that, in the U.S., 4.4 million songbirds are

TOP **TIP**
Teach your cat to enjoy walking on a leash. Take *Cat Fancy* magazine writer Karen Payne's advice—"Don't use a collar, but a sturdy, lightweight figure-eight or figure-H halter with one strap that passes around the cat's neck and another strap that passes around the body behind the forelegs." The harness should fit snugly but shouldn't be too tight. Just hook the leash into the ring in the center above the cat's back and use treats to persuade Kitty Dearest to "come along." At first, just getting used to the harness may take a little while and lots of billing and cooing on your part, but if the harness becomes associated with pleasurable excursions, that shouldn't be too long in coming.

killed *daily* by cats. The number of tiny mammals like mice and rats is even higher. Imagine being captured by a great alien being with eyes the size of Volkswagens and claws like boathooks—think how your tiny heart would pound and you will understand how those small animals feel.

For years, I was terribly stubborn about letting my cats out. After all, nothing bad happened to my cats. They were smart. Then one of my littlest angels, Crystal, a cat I had always told people "never goes anywhere," disappeared.

I searched high and low, the panic of loss growing. How could she have vanished into thin air? I *knew* she hadn't been hit by a car. After all, we lived on a cul-de-sac, a slow road to nowhere where a few cars a day, not counting my neighbors', cruised along slowly, looking out at the river. Anyway, although tiny Crystal would have lost any argument with a 3,000-pound vehicle, she was so wily, so cautious, so clever.

Of course, she *had* been hit. Whether she had lain unconscious for two days or had been too weak to call out, I will never know. On the third day, she found the strength to drag herself home. She must have been so relieved to have made it all the way to the back steps. How long she lay there waiting for me

TOP **TIP**

In places like California where large birds of prey have been known to swoop down and snatch a cat (or take chunks of fur for nesting material), ultra-conscientious cat guardians like Maria Peterson have a solution. Weave a crisscross framework of visible white string across the top of your yard or other exposed areas to deter hawks and their kin, thus keeping Kitty safe and in one piece. Some cats may even tolerate wearing a protective vest when outdoors—this has the added benefit of protecting them from aggressive dogs.

before her end came, I have no idea. I found her there when I came home from work. The vet said her ribs were broken on one side and her lungs had collapsed. I could see that she had lost a great deal of blood, from the size of the gaping hole in her side. I was so angry with myself. I loved Crystal so much, but I had so stupidly allowed my nonchalance, my misplaced confidence, to cause her such pain.

After that, we built a cat run of "non-climbable" fencing stretched over fence posts. Of course, cats being cats, they didn't take this gracefully at first. We had to contend with nasty looks, a bit of screaming and clawing at the doors, and mad dashes through our legs when we dared to set foot outside. Then they settled down. Of course, it would have been far simpler had they never been used to going outside.

We knocked out a small basement panel window and replaced it with a cat flap. Our cat "tribe" soon realized they could go through the flap at will, then play in the dirt, feel the breeze, even lounge about in the sun on a good day. We erected a haphazard structure of orange crates and stumps that allowed them to climb and jump and sun themselves or hide for private naps. This structure proved enormous fun and kept the cats agile and exercised as well as amused. They invented their own version of "Who's the King of the Castle?" and never seemed to tire of amicably lording it over each other.

When I moved into a city apartment, the run was scrapped, but by then I had found all sorts of ways to give my cats only the best of what they would experience outside, with none of the peril.

The modern world is far too dangerous a place for unattended, trusting little lifeforms. Today, I would no more open the door and say, "Go play," to my cats any more than I would to a toddler.

WHAT YOU CAN DO

1 The best news is that if you have a yard or even a patio, you can effectively fence it to keep cats in. Cats can leap over, climb, or

otherwise defeat standard dog fencing, so you will need cat-proof, keep-'em-down-on-the-farm, angle fencing.

It's also pretty easy to convert an IKEA (or similar) bookcase or two into a fabulous outdoor setup. (See PETA.org/Catio.)

You can erect angle wire inward from your fence top, or you can buy a special system, like Cat Fence-In. This is not an electric fence (which I definitely do not recommend) but has a tangle-free net of small mesh that attaches to any existing wood, masonry, wire, or chain-link fence. It is designed to last for many years and won a *Cat Fancy* magazine Editor's Choice award for Best of Cat Products.

My favorite endorsement of Cat Fence-In comes from Sally Daniels of Ann Arbor, who says that her cats, Brady and O'Keefe, who "rule the house with iron paws," use their fenced yard to bask in the sun, watch butterflies, and leap about at night chasing lightning bugs. Says Ms. Daniels, "Are they satisfied? Pur-r-fectly!" For information or to discuss options, visit catfencein.com or call 1-888-738-9099.

2 Spend time outside with your cat. If Kitty is young, she may get used to wearing a harness, and as long as you can stand a slow pace, the two or three of you can stroll. One of my cats, Pandora, used to walk along the C&O Canal with me for about a mile, mewing happily all the way. The sight of her surprised our local muskrat family so much that they forgot all fear and came out onto the bank of the adjacent swamp to gawk at her.

The important thing is to be patient and supportive. Don't pull or tug, just go with the flow (or lack thereof!).

3 Even if you have central air conditioning, install a screen on at least one window and provide a cat seat there to allow your cat to smell the great outdoors—unless she grew up indoors, in which case she will think you have lost your mind and are trying to give her pneumonia.

4 Plant indoor grasses for your cat to nibble on. This can be beneficial to her health, as well as allowing an outdoor

fantasy meal. Grass is a natural laxative. The folic acid in the leaves can help Tiddles vomit up those nasty hairballs that make her an embarrassment at parties. Avoid using chemically treated seeds (often identifiable by their clearly dyed green, red, or blue coloring).

You can plant seeds like oats (easy, cheap, and big), wheat (not wheatgrass), Japanese barnyard millet, bluegrass, and fescue. Alfalfa and bean sprouts should be used only in small amounts, as these may reduce the protein value of other things fed. Those knowledgeable about seeds advise against growing or feeding sorghum or Sudan grass to cats, as these can cause cyanide poisoning. For extra fun, you can even grow catnip indoors!

15
A QUIZ
FOR YOU
FROM YOUR CAT

There they lie, flat on their backs, legs in the air, eyes tightly closed. Are they dreaming of fish or birds? No. They are dreaming of the perfect you. Whenever those whiskers twitch, they are remembering one of your foibles. Like annoying people who get married and then instantly want to reform their new spouse, cats have very firm ideas about what they want in a lifetime companion. They can be excused for feeling that way. After all, they didn't choose you, they got stuck with you. Like mail-order brides, if they had hissed and spat and refused to be carried over the threshold, who knows what would have become of them. They might have ended up in the gutter, forced to sell kittens to motorcycle gangs to support their catnip habit.

So, are you your cat's Prince Charming or Cinderella? Or are you a cat's nightmare, a less-than-ideal guardian and friend, the person who leaves the door open to the nice, warm, cozy dryer and then wonders, too late, what that thumping sound might be? Don't think this can't happen to you unless you are vigilance itself. Ask Jean Lundy, a devoted shelter reformer and taker-in of animal refugees. One afternoon, as she headed up the basement stairs, having pushed the High-Cottons button, she heard a clumpety-clump sound. Her initial thought? How grown-up her son was: finally, actually washing his sneakers! The "sneakers" turned out to be her old tan cat, who lost all the skin on his face and feet—and a little part of his mind—that day.

Tom made a slow and painful recovery but was never quite the same.

This checklist allows you to rate your performance from your cat's perspective and to see if you are the cat's pajamas, the conscientious person who has her cat's safety and well-being in mind at all times. I have omitted a few of my favorite "nevers," such as "Never leave the tops off cleaning fluids or leave antifreeze out." I suppose there is as little point to listing that as to saying, "Never back your car into the garage before opening the door." Such things are mistakes. In the case of antifreeze—which, sadly, must smell, to cats, like cod liver oil or some other exotic and alluring delicacy—an encounter is the worst kind of mistake, a fatal error. This deadly liquid turns to aldehyde in cats' bodies, and they die very badly. Dr. Michael Fox, author of the syndicated column "The Pet Doctor," reports that cats are also drawn to Clorox. Lids on, please.

I probably should also have listed, "Never toilet-train your cat." I know some people swear by such nonsense, but I suspect that they are the same people who insist on torturing ducks and seagulls by throwing bread to a whole flock of them one minuscule piece at a time. It drives the birds nuts, forces them to exert themselves unnecessarily, makes them wonder at the stupidity of our species, and puts them through paces that serve only to show that the bread-thrower is interested in showing off, when all the birds want to do is eat. Not to belabor this point, but someone is bound to suggest the toilet-training idea, which sounds all very well and good if you don't think about it from the cat's perspective. Old, very young, tiny, frail, sick, or heavy cats and those who haven't a good sense of balance (not all cats land on their feet, just as not all Welsh people can sing like canaries) will not thank you for making them haul their frames (or fail to haul them) up and onto a seat of a shape and at a height designed to accommodate a human being's backside.

Give yourself one point for every statement that applies:

The 'Good Guardian' Checklist

1. I have had my cat(s) spayed or neutered.
2. I never let my cat(s) out unattended. (Give yourself two points if you have provided an escape-proof yard or another cat exercise area.)
3. I always keep the litter box impeccably clean.
4. I am always on time with meals.
5. I keep a cat carrier and my veterinarian's number handy.
6. My cat(s) can see out of at least one window without having to behave like a contortionist.
7. I know the signs of cystitis.
8. I take time to play with my cat(s) every day, even on days when I feel bilious, might be fired if I'm late for work (giving you even more time to play with your cat later), or have an important date.
9. I never forget to kiss my cat goodbye when I leave home. (Give yourself two points if you never leave home. See number 8.)
10. I always remember to bring home a present. (This can be as small and inexpensive as a dried leaf or a clod of dirt. The important part is to make an Academy Award–style fuss over the presentation.)
11. I never smoke in the vicinity of my cat's sensitive nostrils.
12. I give my cat fresh water and scrub all bowls at least once a day.
13. I always keep the dryer door closed and check for sleeping cats before switching it on. (Number 13 has proved most unlucky for many a cat, who have lost the pads of their feet or their very life to this appliance.)
14. I have provided for my cat in case of my death. (You can take steps to ensure that your cat will be provided for after your death by naming a cat caretaker in your will. Set aside money in a trust fund or make a direct bequest to a trusted

caregiver. If you can't find a friend or relative you can rely on, you might ask a local charitable organization with acceptable standards to adopt your animal or to place him in a good home, even to guarantee to euthanize him should this be the best alternative. Make sure you leave the organization enough money to care for your cat if that's what you think best and enough leeway to let him go if pain enters his life. If you are still stuck, please call PETA.)

15. There is a sticker on my front door that reads, IN CASE OF FIRE OR OTHER EMERGENCY, PLEASE RESCUE MY [NUMBER] CATS.

16. My cat is microchipped and always correctly attired in detachable neckwear with a current address and contact number tastefully emblazoned thereupon.

17. I would never have my cat declawed. (If your cat came to you declawed, you can still score a point if you are horrified. Score two points if you have tracked down and tried to educate the perpetrator.)

18. I never board my cat away from my home when I go on vacation. (Give yourself two points if you never go on vacation.)

19. I never send my cat to an outside grooming shop. (See chapter 6 for bathing instructions.)

20. I never allow the vet to keep my cat overnight. (You may still take a point if the only exception is in the case of extremely serious injury or illness and the veterinary office is one of those emergency ones that is open and attended all night. There is otherwise no sense in abandoning an already distressed cat to a smelly, strange, usually uncomfortable cage, surrounded by wailing animals, barking dogs, and the pungent smell of disinfectant and other patients' waste. You can look after your own cat in your own bedroom and call

if there's a problem—far quicker, in all probability, than the night caretaker, if your vet actually bothers to employ one.)

21. I would never fly my cat in the cargo hold of a plane.

22. I never make noise when my cat is trying to rest.

23. I never yell or swear at my cat.

24. I never fail to answer if my cat says something to me.

25. I never throw my cat off the bed or any furniture.

26. I would never give my cat away to someone else. (The only excuses here are imprisonment, terminal illness, incapacity, and military dispatch in time of war.)

27. I would never leave children, strangers, or people whose reliability I had not verified in charge of my cat.

28. I would never give my cat an aspirin. (Cats cannot metabolize drugs as we can. Aspirin makes them very ill. Just one Tylenol can kill them.)

HOW DID YOU SCORE?

Only your cat is perfect, but any score below 16 on this basic cat care quiz demands your immediate remedial training. Remember every time you have resolved to eat less fat and then ordered the fries? This is not like that. This is serious business. You must decide immediately to change your stripes. If you don't, your cat will never adore you. I'm surprised you can live with yourself, for that matter. This quiz involves some pretty basic pointers on looking after the mental and physical well-being of your cat(s). If you scored 25 or more, I'll be moving in with you. If you scored 20 or less, you simply have to shape up. Where are you failing? What can you do right away to overcome the problem? Put a note on your dashboard? Make an appointment with the vet? Change a plan? Go to some extra effort?

Whatever it takes, if you do it now, you will have become the very person your cat has been sculpting in his sleep. You will, in fact, be the totally adored man or woman of your cat's dreams.

16
WHAT'S *THAT* IN MY CAT'S FOOD?

Is feeding a cat complicated? Well, it is, and it isn't. But if you think opening a can of cat food is all you have to do to feed your feline, you should think again. After reading this chapter, you could well march into your veterinarian's office and rip those pet food pamphlets to shreds. Just as most physicians don't know beans about human nutrition (in fact, only a handful of medical schools even have a course in it), most vets haven't a clue whether that canned and bagged pet food they recommend has any drawbacks. When I see a vet hand out a free brochure and sample from one of the commercial pet food salespeople and warn their clients away from anything nontraditional, I think about the doctors who, 30 years ago, appeared on TV in white coats to advertise cigarettes. It's enough to make your cat's hair stand on end.

Steel yourself. No matter how attractive the ads and labels, commercial cat food is, by and large, muck. Literally, because cows and chickens are fed their own waste (as well as old newspapers, plastic, cement, and other fillers you wouldn't add to a stew), and figuratively, because pet food comes from animal parts that end up in what are called the "4-D" bins.

Four-D bins are the bins into which slaughterhouse workers pitch animal body parts the government inspectors decide are "not fit for human consumption." The four D's stand for dead, dying, diseased, and disabled. When you read the words "meat byproducts "on the cat food can or bag label, think of skin, hide, hair, beaks, toes, and tail ends.

Meat is often loaded with E. *coli*, salmonella, campylobacter, and other tiny forms of virulent bacteria that give people the stomach flu or kill the occasional consumer, and an impressive four out of five consumers who eat steak and chicken will eventually end up in a soothingly decorated room in the intensive care ward, fighting for their lives after a heart attack, stroke, or cancer. That's one reason I remain of the opinion that *all* meat should end up in the "unfit for human consumption" bins. Nevertheless, the truly revolting bits, such as lungs with ulcerated tumors on them and such unsavory "extras" as ear flaps, nose skin, and toe folds (but, hey, save that yummy liver and tongue!) go into the bins.

What else makes up fancy cat food? Sometimes, it is believed, although the pet food industry denies it but provides no evidence to support the claim—and no regulations forbid it—it contains bits of "recycled" cats and dogs who are "rendered," i.e., melted down in processing plants after their bodies are collected from veterinary hospitals and pounds. Oh, and parts of broken-down horses used for racing, commonly known as deadstock, end up in it, too. And if you think you're missing all that muck when you buy cat food containing "meat meal," think again. Veterinarian Wendell O. Belfield says, "Do you know what is in meat meal? Urine, fecal matter, hair, pus, meat [from animals afflicted] with cancer and T.B., etc."

After a big cook-up, all this mess goes into cans or bags with pretty labels, marked "Little Cleopatra," "Top Veterinarian's Choice," or some other such cute or science-y name. Not only is this "food" revolting, it is also expensive. You could pay NASA to name the next space probe after your cat for the amount of money it takes to vittle up these days.

In the case of commercial cat food, the proof is *not* in the pudding. Cats will eat it. After all, they are true carnivores who, given the chance, will rip a mouse's organs out of his belly with as much relish as Caligula relieving his sister of her baby. Notwithstanding this fact, animals who hunt usually eat the stomach contents of their prey first. Since mice, cats' favorite staple, are vegans, that means cats eat their veggies before they get to the meat portion of the meal.

There are other things to bear in mind as you contemplate the marketing genius of the pet food industry person who first figured out that someone would actually pay money for muck.

For starters, R. Geoffrey Broderick, D.V.M., warns, "Every time a pet trustingly eats another bowl of high-sugar pet food, he is being brought that much closer to diabetes, hypoglycemia, overweight, nervousness, cataracts, allergy and death." It's enough to make you lose your appetite.

The animal feed eaten by the animals who go on to be eaten by your cat is also a pesticide potpourri. Cows are not only *fed* pesticides but also *sprayed* with concentrated doses of them before they go in the truck to the slaughterhouse. Pesticides build up in muscle and tissue (i.e., in meat) and are linked to cancer and other nasty and serious health problems in humans, cats, and other animals.

Farmed animals, who are nowadays granted the privilege of only a brief glimpse of life while incarcerated in small cages or stalls, are no longer made of wholesome mother's milk, sunshine, fresh air, and lush pastures. To make sure profits are maximized, most animals unlucky enough to be used for food are kept indoors for most or all of their lives, fed an artificial diet (see above), injected with drugs, given hormones, sprayed with chemicals, and so on. All this is to make them put on weight fast, to break down adrenaline produced by the fear and stress they live in, and to attempt to curb the diseases that run rampant through the crowded "intensive farming units." Much of what is put into and on them is passed on through their flesh to the consumer. And the most unappetizing, disease-ridden parts are saved for you-know-who. In the case of cat food, the consumer is, of course, your cat.

If you are a vegetarian or vegan for ethical reasons, you may have been wondering how you can justify supporting the slaughterhouse. If anyone tells you the pet food market is inconsequential to the meat industry, you can assure them that it is as consequential as leather goods (i.e., very consequential). Anyone who has priced a pair of leather pumps or a month's supply of canned cat food realizes that there's big money in them thar "byproducts." When we buy meat-based pet food, we continue to make it profitable to allow heifers and hens to lie mangled and ignored in their pens and on the ramps to the killing floor. Meat stinks—not only for them but also for cat health, the environment, and all of us.

So do you have to cook for your cat? Well, no, because there are some wholesome processed foods, such as veggie burgers. There are certainly lots of "people foods" that cats love. But if you want your cat to be around for a long, long time, yes, you might make tracks for the kitchen. Cooking for your cat, as for any other family member, is loving and thoughtful, and it's good for your cat's health. In fact, I'll include recipes at the end of this chapter that may convince you that, just as you don't have to cook for yourself from scratch, there may be nothing more difficult to this way of life than simply opening a can and mixing a few things together. However, be forewarned: A cat's dietary needs are different from those of a dog or a human being, so if you are going to take charge of your cat's diet, you must know what essential nutrients your cat requires.

For example, the amino acid taurine, which is vital to a cat's growth and well-being, is an excellent case in point. The first cases of taurine deficiency were discovered not in vegan cats but in cats eating strictly meat-based canned foods. Taurine is destroyed by cooking, it was discovered, so cats who eat cooked meat must be fed supplemental, synthetic taurine, just like vegan cats. The only surefire way to avoid having to add synthetic supplements like taurine to a cat's food is to feed them raw meats, but this has its own drawbacks, considering the rampant contamination of today's meat supply with such dangerous bacteria as those mentioned above. However, thanks to the God of Commerce, synthetic taurine supplements are easy to get.

One cat to point to is Teresa Chagrin's beautiful, black, long-haired cat, Yoko. Yoko was featured in *The Wall Street Journal*, whose reporter found her tucking into "garbanzo beans, lentils, split peas, and broccoli—with a pinch of garlic." She also "nibbles on asparagus spears" on special occasions. Having met Yoko, I know that she also loves tofu, bean soups, and pasta. Teresa makes sure her beloved cat, whom she adopted from a Washington shelter, gets lots of protein. She also feeds Yoko a supplement called Vegecat that ensures she has enough taurine.

Another ardent "veggie cat" person who runs a rescue shelter for cat waifs feeds her orphans a strict vegan diet for health and ethical reasons. These lucky strays enjoy cantaloupe (most cats like all sorts of melons), cucumbers, chickpeas, cooked potato, fake hot dogs, and a variety of other veggie foods rich in protein and vitamins.

If you try to teach an old cat new cat food tricks, he may do what my cat Jarvis did and walk right through the home cooking that I had lovingly prepared for him, not even recognizing it as food! If there is anyone I'd listen to on dealing with this sort of challenge, it is Alisa Mullins, a PETA senior staff writer. Alisa advises people new to all this that the way to wean a cat off commercial cat food is to mix veggies in with your cat's regular food and then gradually diminish the amount of commercial food in the mix.

Alisa recommends starting out with veggie burger recipes, because most cats seem to love them. She uses the kind made from soy or wheat gluten that, like so many vegan burgers and mince nowadays, really do taste like meat. Since the mid-1990s, when veggie Boca Burgers became a White House favorite, many brands have become available in most supermarkets, Beyond Burger being my current favorite. They can be mashed or crumbled after cooking and used as the basis of other recipes for cats. When Amy Barnes' cat, Rita, discovered veggie fajitas (made from tempeh), she never looked back.

Alisa also recommends sprinkling a little baby food (not the kind with onion powder, which may cause anemia in cats), nutritional (not brewer's) yeast, or even dry catnip on top of a finicky eater's portion. She had to sneak the peas, carrots, and other veggies into one of her cat's food but reports that fresh, steamed veggies go over better than the canned kind with her cats.

A conscientious cat mom, Alisa adds half a clove of garlic per cat per day, which she mashes in the food processor. She also adds herbs like parsley, sage, and rosemary once in a while (fresh preferably, dried sometimes) and always mixes in digestive enzymes, rosehips powder (a natural source of vitamin C, which helps reduce the risk of getting cystitis), plus alfalfa, which is full of vitamins and minerals and a natural diuretic. Phew! The recipes at the end are actually quite simple.

While we're destroying myths about cat food, let's not forget milk. Most cats are actually lactose intolerant when it comes to trying to digest cow's milk and can get runny stools, upset tummies, and congestion from it.

TOP **TIP**

Before cats found their human families, they had to hunt for their supper. All that stalking and pouncing burned off calories. That makes pre-mealtime an ideal time to get a fat cat to stretch a leg. Show Kitty the food, but then get her accustomed to playing "chase the tin foil ball," "jump for the moon," or some other strenuous game before you serve up the meal.

Don't forget to look in the Recommended Reading section of this book for more sources of information on health and diet.

A word about weight control: Be honest. Does your cat look like one of those old wartime blimps? A sort of cross between a cat and a couch? Is she a potential challenger to 46-pound Himmy, an Australian cat who got so fat he had to be ferried about in a wheelbarrow?

If that's the case, and we all know that Spanx and Stairmasters aren't going to do the trick for her (although the more you play with your cats, the more fat they'll burn off), it's probably time to look at what she's stoking up on. Obesity is a health problem. Cats, like human beings, shorten their life spans when they widen their waistlines. All that fat stressing their hearts and lungs is not a good thing. Dr. Michael Fox has more good advice to offer. He says that "pet foods are very palatable and low in bulk (fiber), so the animal's appetite is stimulated, but a satisfying feeling of fullness is never achieved." That's why our cats always seem hungry.

Here are Dr. Fox's tips:
• Never leave dry food out overnight.
• Divide up what they would normally eat at 4 p.m. into three soft-food meals: morning, afternoon, and evening. Do this for a week, then start substituting more and more boiled rice for their regular soft food. Season the rice with a little Marmite, Vegemite, or vegetable bouillon. Work up to three parts rice to one part soft food only.

Here's another pointer: Remove food between meals. In nature, cats aren't served cafeteria-style. Their gastric juices have to flow, their adrenaline has to surge, and fasting from one meal to the next means that the energy and the biological matter used for digestion are now freed up to do good work in other ways. A free availability of food can cause a finicky eating syndrome and other things beginning with the letter F (i.e., fatness).

VITAL SUPPLEMENTS

Vegecat products are made by a company committed to providing cats (and dogs) with pure food. You can prepare the suggested meals in your own kitchen once a week using the sort of ingredients, such as organic garbanzo beans, gluten flour, and yeast, available at any health food store. Once you've prepared the mix, you just add Vegecat powder to meet your cat's complete nutritional needs.

Vegecat does provide kibble recipes for an extra measure of convenience, which the recipes listed in this section are adapted from, and my cats love the stuff. The methods are outlined in detailed instructions accompanying each container of the supplement. It takes about 30 minutes to make 10 days' worth of kibble, and other recipes are even shorter.

Kittens up to 12 months old require *Vegekit*. If you have both kittens and older cats, you can feed them all Vegekit. Vegecat does seem to make cats' coats shine, and because there is no rotting meat in any of the food, an added bonus is less smelly cat feces—something you can't help but appreciate.

Vegecat can be ordered online at PETA.org/Vegecat, where you'll also find great cat food recipes, or call 406-295-4944.

VegeYeast is a powdered supplement made from nutritional yeast that is specially processed and pH-adjusted for finicky cats, which is 80% of all cats alive at any given time. Because cats have a preference for acidic products and because of the importance of keeping urine acidic, this product is a good choice. It can be used in all the Vegekit recipes. Dogs like it, too.

As for commercial cat food, I'd suggest these two brands: Evolution vegan cat kibble and canned food and Wysong Corporation vegan cat kibble.

HOME COOKING FOR THE CAT YOU LOVE: RECIPES

Kittens (up to 12 months old) have mineral and vitamin requirements different from adult cats and need—yes, absolutely need—Vegekit. For cats prone to feline urologic syndrome, avoid whole grains and try adding 500 milligrams of ascorbic acid (vitamin C) per day to meals. It can help prevent infection and acidify the urine. Seitan, gluten flour, seaweed vegetables, yeast, and tofu (use the kind coagulated with calcium sulfate, not nigari, which contains too much magnesium) can all be found in natural food stores. Choose oils from the following group: olive, high oleic (not regular) safflower, peanut, sunflower, or sesame.

13-DAY VEGEKIBBLE

This is my favorite recipe for convenience and palatability. It's very flexible, since many toppings are possible for flavor variations, and most cats take to it well. Once the routine of making kibble is established, you'll find it easy and well worth the initial learning stage.

1 cup corn flour

½ cup defatted soy flour

3 ¼ cups gluten flour

¼ cup wheat germ

¾ cup yeast powder

½ cup Vegecat

¼ cup baking powder

½ Tbsp. salt (if not added before) or ⅛ cup soy or tamari sauce

½ cup oil

1 small can tomato paste (optional)

3 cups water or broth (as necessary)

- Preheat the oven to 325°F (160°C).
- Mix together all the dry ingredients.
- Add the oil, tomato paste (if using), and water or broth to the dry-ingredient mixture.
- Flour your hands and counter and knead into a dough. Taking half the dough, roll out to a thickness of about ½ inch. Place on a cookie sheet. Repeat with the other half of the dough. Place the sheets on the upper rack in the oven and bake for 20 minutes.
- Remove from the oven. Flip each over onto a fresh cookie sheet.
- Bake for 20 minutes more. Remove from the oven and cool slightly. Place on a cutting board. Using a large slightly curved knife, cut horizontally into three strips then cut each of those strips into quarters. Cut each resulting square into kibble-size pieces (like a miniature checkerboard) by cutting first in one direction then the other.
- Place kibble in a warm oven (about 200°F) for 2 to 3 hours until dry and crunchy.
- Store in a covered container. No refrigeration needed.

GARBANZO-SOY 10-DAY RECIPE

4½ cups canned garbanzo beans
1½ cups crumbled veggie burger or 2 cups tofu
½ cup yeast powder, plus more for topping
½ cup oil
1 tsp. salt or 4 tsp. soy sauce
¼ cup Vegecat Seasonings

- Drain the garbanzo beans thoroughly and crush them in a food processor.
- Stir in the remaining ingredients.
- Sprinkle with yeast before serving.

LENTIL-SOY 10-DAY RECIPE

1¾ cups uncooked lentils

1¾ cups textured vegetable protein

¾ cup yeast powder, plus more for topping

¾ cup oil

1 tsp. salt or ¼ cup soy sauce

¼ cup Vegecat Seasonings

- Cook the lentils until just soft.
- Thoroughly drain and add the remaining ingredients.
- Let the textured vegetable protein soften in the mixture before serving.
- Sprinkle with yeast before serving.

You can entice even the finickiest cat with "proprietary yeasts" like the Vegecat brand used as a flavor enhancer. Others are available online.

17
NATURAL REMEDIES FOR KITTY

Some plants hurt, while others heal. That's the difference between "flower remedies"—the application of the oldest medicines and pick-me-ups in history, born of forest lore—and plants that use their natural defenses, like poisons secreted from their leaves, to ward off attacks by cats and other marauding non-plants.

THE CURATIVE POWER OF FLOWERS

Cats need not only smell the roses—they can eat them, too. Two friends, Hilly Beavan and Anthony Lawrence, never leave home without a bottle of Bach's Rescue Remedy, a mixture of flowers including impatiens and clematis, which produces calming, stabilizing effects when cats and other animals experience stress.

More "rat people" than "cat people," Hilly and Ant have been heavily romanced by two white Norway rats who took refuge in their home after the trauma of laboratory life. They gained respect for the contents of Bach's little bottle when they saw its effect in helping the rats "get normal again." They have since tried it on larger whiskered beings and swear that, whatever the incident or accident, you should always bring out the Bach's.

"It works," says Hilly, "for just about anything, including a run-in with a collie or a car, for insect bites and cat fights, trips to the vet, and just about anything ugly that could befall a poor cat."

Bach's Original Flower Remedies were first composed in 1930 by Dr. Edward Bach, an English physician who found that if patient stress is left unresolved, it inevitably leads to physical disorder. He put together 38 remedies that are not only harmless (harsh drugs are not among the ingredients) but also gentle and, many believe, impressively effective.

The many testimonials in *Bach Flower Remedies for Animals* (see Recommended Reading) echo Hilly and Ant's experience. For example, G.S. Khalsa, a Michigan physician, writes, "I was visiting a veterinarian friend of mine when another friend brought in a cat who appeared to be quite exhausted. The cat had been out in the rain all day and was frightened. We gave him one dose of Rescue Remedy and, within five minutes, the cat was purring, cozy, and friendly." No wonder some people take a little dose at the end of a workday from hell.

A few drops in a teaspoon of water, drizzled onto the tongue or popped into drinking water, and a traumatized cat feels more sedate and able to cope with what life may offer next.

Bach's remedies aren't only for major traumas. If you have a cat who is jealous, irritable, afraid, or dealing with a distressing experience, such as a household move, travel sickness, or a new baby in the family, there may be a flower remedy that can help. There are websites discussing Bach flower remedies, with FAQs and consultation services that can be handy, at BachFlower.com and BachFlowerPets.com.

Among the remedies most recommended for cats are these:

• **Aspen.** For cats who slink from place to place out of fear, never completely at ease and startling at sounds. (If you suspect past human-caused abuse, Star of Bethlehem is recommended. If you suspect current human-caused abuse, call the humane society.)

• **Beech.** For the cat who has no tolerance for other animals or certain people. A great icebreaker that came in handy in the case of a diplomat's Siamese who used to hide under the couch and then bite into visiting dignitaries' ankles. It is used with Walnut to assist in keeping the peace between two cats who are always at each other's throats.

- **Calming Essence.** For car trips, accidents, illness, injury; during a long absence; before and after surgery; for any extreme stress.
- **Chicory.** Helps stabilize the emotions of an extremely jealous cat. This is a very helpful remedy when you are trying to introduce another cat into the family and your cat has turned green.
- **Clematis.** For anytime a cat appears stunned or experiences unusual patterns of sleeping beyond the typical catnap. Used in helping regain consciousness after an accident or operation.
- **Honeysuckle.** It's not only "hep cats" who get the blues. This remedy can be helpful for a grieving cat who has lost someone close to him/her and feels depressed and alone.
- **Larch.** Can help the lowest-ranking cat—the runt, for example—gain self-confidence and become more emotionally balanced.
- **Mimulus.** Helps cats overcome fear of thunderstorms, Wagnerian music, vacuum cleaners, trips to the vet, the encroachment of screaming children, and other worries.
- **Star of Bethlehem.** For all trauma, past and present, physical and psychological. For recuperation from surgery, injury, boarding, and other nasty occurrences that affect a cat's dignity, freedom, health, or security.

TOP **TIP**

No need for your home to be plantless. Cats can have a little chew on the following plants, *without* causing you heart failure:

- Begonias
- Coleus
- Spleenwort (Don't you hope it tastes better than it sounds?)
- Ti plant
- Wandering Jew
- Prayer plant
- Dracaena
- Succulents like jade plant, donkey's tail, and coral beads

Take a look in the Reading and Handy Resources sections of this book for information on flower essence companies, such as Anaflora, a company that provides 26 formulas that address the "physical, mental, emotional, and spiritual needs" of animals and will send a free brochure on its products.

HERBS AND HOMEOPATHY

Veterinarians who practiced homeopathy used to be as scarce as hens' teeth. Now they're not hard to find.

Most not only use plant extracts or herbal medicine to try to cure what ails a cat, when such treatment is considered appropriate, but also look at other methods that take into consideration the whole cat.

Such veterinarians, many of whom join the American Holistic Veterinary Medical Association, find that homeopathic treatments can sometimes do the job when conventional veterinary medicine (allopathy) has failed, and at other times such methods work well in tandem with traditional medicine. For example, Dr. Richard Pitcairn, considered the longtime leading homeopathic veterinarian in the U.S. (now retired), advises cat owners to use symphytum to help heal fractures. It is made from the comfrey plant and used to be called "knit-bone" long, long ago—a dead giveaway that it is believed to aid in the healing of broken bones.

I favor always consulting a veterinarian, but among the homeopathic treatments that I have heard favorable reports on are those used for arthritis and for relief from itching and allergies.

If you go to a homeopathic vet, don't be surprised to hear questions about your cat's preferences for a sleeping place and how he relates to others of all species in the household as well as sundry oddball questions, the answers to which may give important clues about what is going on mentally and physically.

Some homeopaths use other alternative techniques, now routinely available to human patients, such as acupuncture (which can be wonderful for joint pain), Chinese herbal medicine, and chiropractic. I'll let Ulla Davis's story about her cat, Cuchuma, tell the tale:

Cuchuma was being given high doses of cortisone and painkillers because of trouble with his back. The otherwise healthy 10-year-old could no longer get up onto Davis' lap, something that caused both cat and human great sadness.

Davis took her cat to Dr. Raymond Deiter, a holistic veterinarian in Sausalito, California, for an acupuncture treatment. "At the first treatment, he didn't do anything when the doctor put the needles in," Davis told Melinda Sacks of the San Jose Mercury News. "He just put his little face on my arm and went to sleep."

Cuchuma had five treatments over a five-week period and can now get up and down from his bed easily.

PLANT GOT YOUR CAT'S TONGUE?

Some of our most popular houseplants are poisonous and can damage an unsuspecting cat. I recommend an inventory of the household greenery and a quick check when you consider buying a new plant.

Luckily, most cats don't seem to feel the urge to chew on North America's favorite hanging, dangling plant, the philodendron. Even if you are not a heart surgeon, you will be able to recognize the shape of the leaves on this plant, which is also known as heart-leaf because no one sat up all night thinking of something more complicated to call it. The leaves may look cute and romantic, but like Mata Hari, they will betray you: Inside, they contain needlelike crystals of poisonous acid.

Should a cat sink her teeth into a philodendron, the acid mixes with her saliva and makes her mouth, throat, and tongue burn worse than a chili dinner. Jack, one of the PETA cats, found this out the hard way, having discovered a philodendron left as a gift for the hardworking staff in our Research & Investigations Department. His screams were enough to get the whole 4th floor running to his aid.

Jack subsequently lost all interest in horticulture, and the plant was whisked away forever.

Another popular plant is the dieffenbachia, or mother-in-law plant, which has large, oblong leaves painted with light white splotches. This, too, contains acid that causes burning and can make a cat's tongue and throat swollen and terribly painful. If the tongue swells too much, it can block the cat's throat and cause suffocation, necessitating an emergency race to the vet. Sap from the dieffenbachia can cause eye problems, such as inflammation.

Hydrangea is bad, too. It comes in large and small bushes and has very pretty clusters of blue, white, or pink flowers. It can cause stomach cramps, gastrointestinal disturbance, bloody diarrhea, and problems of the heart, lungs, and kidneys.

Forget caladium, with its flashy, bright, heart-shaped leaves in combinations of green, white, orange, and red. It causes burning and pain to the tongue, throat, and mouth. Again, suffocation is possible should the cat's tongue swell to block his throat.

And most ivy is out. As attractive as these climbing plants are with their petite leaves, often green-flecked or edged with white, the small berries on many varieties are extremely dangerous and cause inflammation of the throat and stomach, if swallowed.

Also on the "don't bring home or the cat gets it" list are these:
• Amaryllis
• Arrowhead vine
• Asparagus fern
• Azalea
• Bird of paradise
• Boston ivy
• Cherry
• Chrysanthemum
• Creeping Charlie
• Creeping fig

- Daffodil
- Elephant ears
- Emerald duke
- English holly
- Iris
- Jerusalem cherry
- Marble queen
- Mistletoe
- Pot mum
- Red princess
- Rubber plants
- Schefflera
- Spider mum
- Spider plant
- Sprengeri fern
- Tulip
- Weeping fig

Phew! (That's not a plant, just an expression.)

WHAT TO DO IN A POISONING EMERGENCY

Contact the Pet Poison Control Helpline, 24 hours a day, at PETA.org/PetPoisonHelp or 1-855-764-7661 or the 24/7 ASPCA Animal Poison Control Center at 1-888-426-4435 or PETA.org/ASPCApoisoncontrol.

Get your cat to a vet by helicopter, fast car, or any way you can. If you can reach a veterinarian for advice, they may prescribe activated charcoal or other ways of dealing with the emergency. If you are in a cabin in the woods and have a flat tire during a blizzard, Darlene Polachic, a writer for *Cat Fancy* magazine, advises this:

If your cat has eaten a plant that does *not* cause throat irritation, try to get your cat to vomit. Fill a syringe or baster with one of the following:

- Lukewarm soapy water
- Hydrogen peroxide mixed with an equal amount of lukewarm water
- A teaspoon of salt dissolved in a cup of water
- A teaspoon of mustard powder mixed with a cup of lukewarm water

Squirt the solution down the cat's throat.

If that doesn't work, try to bind the poison to slow its absorption. Feed the cat a mixture of vegetable oil, milk (soy or any kind), and egg whites if you have them. Follow the treatment with a laxative or warm-water enema.

This does not sound like a fun way to spend even five minutes. Removing even the prettiest of poisonous plants to solve the problem before it happens is a far better idea. And the latest news about poinsettia, once thought to be poisonous, is that it isn't. Sadly, I must inform my cats that the news on chocolate is that it still is … for them.

HOLISTIC VETERINARY RESOURCES

The International Veterinary Acupuncture Society
PETA.org/IVAS
P.O. Box 271458
Fort Collins, CO 80527
970-266-0666
office@ivas.org

American Veterinary Chiropractic Association
PETA.org/AVCA
442236 E. 140 Rd.
Bluejacket, OK 74333
918-784-2231
avcainfo@junct.com

Pitcairn Institute of Veterinary Homeopathy
PETA.org/PIVH
760-230-4784
info@pivh.org

Academy of Veterinary Homeopathy
PETA.org/AVH
P.O. Box 232282
Leucadia, CA 92023-2282
1-866-652-1590

American Holistic Veterinary Medical Association
PETA.org/AHVMA
P.O. Box 630
Abingdon, MD 21009
410-569-0795
office@ahvma.org

American Academy of Veterinary Acupuncture
PETA.org/AAVA
P.O. Box 803
Fayetteville, TN 37334
931-438-0238
office@aava.org

Veterinary Medical Aromatherapy Association
PETA.org/VMAA
6315 S. Rainbow Blvd., Ste. 104
Las Vegas, NV 89118
702-381-0710

American College of Veterinary Botanical Medicine
PETA.org/ACVBM
9002 Sunset Dr.
Colden, NY 14033-9610

Veterinary Botanical Medicine Association
PETA.org/VBMA
6410 Hwy. 92
Acworth, GA 30102
office@vbma.org

RECOMMENDATIONS

CHARITIES

Alley Animals, Inc.

P.O. Box 27487

Towson, MD 21285-7487

410-823-0899

www.alleyanimals.org

Get out the tissues if you dare read this marvelous group's newsletter. Local to Baltimore, Maryland, this plucky band of volunteers plies the endless labyrinth of alleyways, abandoned houses, and drug-dealer hangouts, rescuing those poor cats society has truly cast out. Sometimes, they are too late, as with "Little Innocent One," excerpted here from the Alley Animals news bulletin:

> The night started off quietly for us as we began our route through the alleys (although the night is never quiet or peaceful for the animals struggling to survive there). But I was about to be taken by a whirlwind of emotion when I pulled into an alleyway and saw a kitten lying

on the cement in front of the car. I said to myself, "My God, I hope she's still alive." I jumped out to retrieve her.

Before I picked her up I knew she was dead, but she had not been so for long, the blood from her limp body on my hands, still moist. As I carried her body back to the car, I could hardly contain my anger. I wanted to shout out, "Who did this! Where are you hiding? Come out to face me and the crime you committed against this innocent one. Come out from hiding, coward."

I could plainly see all the "fun" that was had in the wicked ugly things done to her. She had to have been friendly to allow herself to be handled—a wild kitten instinctively knows not to trust humans. All she hoped for was a little kindness, maybe something to eat. Instead, she was hung with a clothesline and, the many jagged rips in her skin told me, thrown to the dogs.
I could only imagine what she had gone through, a friendly kitten trusting the wrong person who repaid this act of innocence by torturing her unspeakably. I want you to look at her and remember that this is why we are fighting so hard to get these animals off the streets.

All donations are gratefully received and put to good use.

People for the Ethical Treatment of Animals (PETA)
PETA.org
501 Front St.
Norfolk, VA 23510
757-622-7382
Info@peta.org
PETA has stopped cat experiments in various laboratories, spays and neuters cats for low to no cost in the U.S. and overseas, and responds

to calls of cruelty and emergencies 24/7, all over the world. It is an international nonprofit, vegan, animal protection organization dedicated to establishing and defending the rights of all animals. With more than 9 million members and supporters globally, PETA entities work through public education, research and investigations, grassroots organizing, litigation, and media campaigns to expose and eliminate animal abuse wherever it occurs.

Whatever you are looking for, and not just about cats, PETA will try to help you find it.

Project Cat, Inc. (New York)
https://www.projectcat.org/
845-687-4983

Your Local Open-Admission Animal Shelter
Please consider helping the wonderful people who rescue, shelter, adopt out, rehome, and euthanize (as they must—"no-kill" shelters close their doors to those who are in need of end-of-life services) cast-off animals. Their work is hard, thankless, and never-ending.

READING

Books for Adults
Some of these books are only available used online but are well worth it.

The Allergic Pet: Holistic Solutions to End the Allergy Epidemic in Our Dogs and Cats
by Deva Khalsa, V.M.D.

Bach Flower Remedies for Animals
by Helen Graham and Gregory Vlamis

Bach Flower Remedies for Animals: The Definitive Guide to Treating Animals
With the Bach Remedies
by Stefan Ball, Judy Ramsell Howard

Bach Flower Remedies for Cats
by Martin Scott and Gael Mariani

Cat Body, Cat Mind: Exploring Your Cat's Consciousness and Total Well-Being
by Michael Fox

Cat Daddy
by Jackson Galaxy

Cat Facts: The Pet Parents A-Z Home Care Encyclopedia: Kitten to Adult, Disease &
Prevention, Cat Behavior Veterinary Care, First Aid, Holistic Medicine
by Amy Shojai

Catification: Designing a Happy and Stylish Home for Your Cat (and You!)
by Jackson Galaxy and Kate Benjamin

Catio Building Tips & Tricks from the Pros for the DIYer
by Don and Yvette Bacha

The Cats' House
by Bob Walker

Cat Wars: The Devastating Consequences of a Cuddly Killer
by Peter P. Marra and Chris Santella

The Doctor's Book of Home Remedies for Dogs and Cats
by the editors of Prevention Magazine

Dr. Pitcairn's Complete Guide to Natural Health for Dogs & Cats
by Richard H. Pitcairn and Susan Hubble Pitcairn

The First-Aid Companion for Dogs & Cats
by Amy Shojai

First Aid for Cats: An Owner's Guide to a Happy Healthy Pet
by Stefanie Schwartz

The Healing Touch: The Proven Massage Program for Cats and Dogs
by Dr. Michael W. Fox

Homeopathic First Aid for Animals: Tales and Techniques From a Country Practitioner
by Kaetheryn Walker

Is Your Cat Crazy? Solutions From the Casebook of a Cat Therapist
by John C. Wright

New Choices in Natural Healing for Dogs & Cats: Herbs, Acupressure, Massage,
Homeopathy, Flower Essences, Natural Diets, Healing Energy
by Amy Shojai

The North American Flower Essences for Pets
by Laura Cutullo

Pet Allergies: Remedies for an Epidemic
by Alfred Plechner and Martin Zucker

A Street Cat Named Bob and How He Saved My Life
by James Bowen

The Trainable Cat: A Practical Guide to Making Life Happier for You and Your Cat
by John Bradshaw and Sarah Ellis

Why Cats Paint: A Theory of Feline Aesthetics
by Heather Busch and Burton Silver

Why Does My Cat Do That? Answers to the 50 Questions Cat Lovers Ask
by Catherine Davidson

Books for Children

Duncan and Dolores
by Barbara Samuels (Simon & Schuster Children's Books)
A child learns to curb some of her more smothering tendencies and wins the affection of her cat.

Fiona Finds Love
by Rhonda Lucas Donald (Who Chains You)
A stray cat faces the dangers of life outdoors on her own with her babies.

The Happy Tale of Two Cats
by Cathy M. Rosenthal (Pet Pundit Publishing)
One family truly cares for their cat and another family doesn't treat their cat well, and she escapes.

Kamie Cat's Terrible Night
by Sheila Hamanaka (Animal Welfare Institute)
A cat gets lost and yearns to be home.

Kids Can Save the Animals! 101 Easy Thing to Do
by Ingrid Newkirk
New York: Warner Books.

This book gives kids lots of facts about animals, animal-friendly companies, and projects and ideas that show how they can help save all creatures great and small.

Lost and Found Cat: The True Story of Kunkush's Incredible Journey
by Doug Kuntz and Amy Shrodes (Crown Books for Young Readers)
Kunkush, a cat, is separated from his refugee family. Compassionate people throughout the world help to reunite them.

The Super Crazy Cat Dance
by Aron Nels Steinke (Blue Apple Books, 2010)
Cats of all shapes, sizes, and colors inspire a little girl to create a crazy dance.

HANDY RESOURCES

Useful Websites

- CatFriendly.com

   Powered by feline veterinarians, Cat Friendly Homes is dedicated to cat caregivers who want to provide the very best care for their cat.

- CatScratching.com

   This site is all about not declawing, why cats need to scratch, finding the right scratching post for your cat, trimming nails, and more.

- IndoorPet.OSU.edu/cats

   The Ohio State University College of Veterinary Medicine has an "Indoor Pet Initiative," which includes a whole page of resources for keeping indoor cats healthy and happy.

- LittleBigCat.com

   Holistic feline health, nutrition, and behavior information

Cat Health

Fresh organic greens are easy to grow, and kits and seeds are on the internet or at most pet supply stores. Avoid any pet stores that sell animals, as they are fueling the trade in breeding while animals in shelters sit looking out of their cages, with hope in their hearts.

Keep a feline first aid kit handy. Most are inadequate, so it's best to stock up for that evacuation during a flood, fire, earthquake, or hurricane or for when Kitty is ill. Emergency Zone and E.R. Cat Survival are among the companies providing the basics. Always have a carrier ready for any emergency.

For cat massage, see the books section above, and there's this also: Tellington TTouch® for Happier, Healthier Cats DVD and TTouch® of Magic for Cats DVD, available to order at PETA.org/CatMassage.

Food and Treats

• **Benevo**
  PETA.org/BenevoCatFood
  Offers vegan kibble and canned food

• **PETA DIY cat treat ideas**
  PETA.org/PETADIYcattreat

• **PETA online food feature**
  "PETA's Complete Guide to Vegan Dog and Cat Food"

• **Vegecat**
  PETA.org/VegecatSupplements
  Vegan supplements for making homemade food

• **Wysong**
  PETA.org/WysongCatFood
  Offers vegan kibble, also sells meat-based food

Catios

Custom-made tunnels and "catios" can be had for the adventurous or reclusive cat.

- **The Cattopia**
  PETA.org/CattopiaQuote
  720-201-0591

- **DIY version**
  PETA.org/Catio
  Seattle and Portland may again offer tours of the various wonderful catios in their cities to give people ideas of what they might want to build themselves at home in order to let their cats enjoy fresh air and sunshine, while still keeping them and wildlife safe. These links are inspiring and helpful, even for folks who don't go on the tours.

- **Digital DIY tips**
  PETA.org/HellaCustomCatio
  Paperback and ebook versions are available from Amazon.

Cat Adventure

- **Kittywalk.com**
  1-877-548-8905
  kittywalk5@optonline.net

- **Target**
  Cat leash and harness sets

- **PetSafe**
  "Come With Me Kitty" Harness and Bungee Leash adjustable cat leash and harness sets

- **Mr. Peanuts Premium Products**
  PETAMall.com/Specialty

Mr. Peanuts is a cruelty-free lifestyle brand with a mission promoting animal welfare. It actively donates to rescues, shelters, and animal welfare organizations and focuses on environmentally friendly, ethically produced, top-quality products.

Cat Furniture

For safe ways for cats to run high up, alongside the walls and just under the ceiling, or sleep and hang out from above.

• **Alpha Paw**
PETA.org/AlphaPawRamp
Ramps of all kinds, including ones designed for arthritic cats or others with trouble getting about

• **PetSafe**
PETA.org/PetSafeStairs
Cool cat stairs

• **Homethangs Catwalk**
PETA.org/Homethangcatwalk
Great catwalk plans and designs

All kinds of cat furniture are widely available at Amazon, Walmart, Target, Etsy, and other stores. Here are some helpful Etsy shops:

• **CatWallFurniture**
Wall-mounted cat furniture, beds, shelves, and feeders

• **HexHouzCatFurniture**
All products are handmade in this family-owned business.

• **MeowMakerDesigns**
Caves, beds, scratchers and perches

- **NewCatHorizons**

  Elegant yet simple wall-mounted furniture for cats

- **TheCatLadderStore**

  Custom cat ladders

- **Thenerdycathome**

  Furniture-protecting cat scratchers

Cat Toys

- **Cat Dancer Products**

  PETA.org/CatDancer

  Offers toys and scratching pads

- **Cat's Meow**

  PETA.org/CatsMeowToy

  This motorized toy is available from Walmart and Amazon.

- **Cosmic Pet Products**

  CosmicPet.com

  Cosmic Pet is an industry leader in the production of innovative and stimulating pet toys and accessories.

- **Floppy Fish**

  PETA.org/Floppyfish

  Available from Bed Bath & Beyond, Amazon, and other retailers

- **PETA DIY cat toy ideas**

  PETA.org/PETADIYcattoy.

  These don't require lots of skills or money.

Catnip
- **Kong**

  PETA.org/KongCatnip

  Kong offers catnip flakes, spray, and toys as well as other items for cats, including tunnels, scratchers, and laser pointers.

- **Mountain Rose Herbs**

  PETA.org/MountainRoseHerbs

  Company policy about organics and sustainability: https://info. mountainroseherbs.com/organics-sustainability#fair

- **The Cat House**

  PETA.org/CatHouseHoneySuckle

  Sells honeysuckle products for cats

Cat Videos
- **Amazon Prime**

  PETA.org/MoviesforCats

  Titles include "Forest Songbirds" and "Chipmunk vs. Corn Cob."

- **YouTube**

  PETA.org/TVforCats

  Videos can be watched on a computer or cast to television.

Stain Removers
- **PETA's Cruelty-Free Guide**

  PETA.org/CFstainremover

  A great resource for cleaning products and stain remover that's updated regularly

- **Nature's Miracle Stain and Odor Remover**

  www.Natures-miracle.com

  Available from Target and other big-box stores

Dealing With Grief

Intense feelings of grief over the death of a loved one are normal and natural. Should it matter whether the loved one is a human being or a cherished member of another species? No. Grief is grief.

- **PETA.org/PETAGriefGuide**
  Comforting words and handy guides to books and counseling

- **Pet Loss Partners**
  PETA.org/PETALossPartners

Ways to Help Other Cats

- **AmazonSmile**
  Smile.Amazon.com
  Select PETA as your benefiting charity and AmazonSmile will donate 0.5% of the cost of your eligible purchases to PETA whenever you make them through AmazonSmile.

- **Animal-friendly checks**
  PETAMall.com/Specialty
  Why use a boring bank check when you can make a difference for animals every time you pay a bill? Funds raised from sales of the checks fund animal protection work. Choose from a variety of animal-friendly check and mailing-label designs, or customize your own. Ten percent of the purchase price of PETA Checks will be donated to PETA.

- **Volunteer at your local shelter.**
  Play with the cats, foster if possible, find homes, and do anything else you can to help.